English Skills 4

Answers

Carol Matchett

Schofield & Sims

WHICH BOOK?

The **English Skills** books are aligned with the end-of-year objectives for Key Stage 2. For the majority of pupils aged 7 to 11, follow the guidance given on page 2 as to which book to use with each year group.

If a pupil is working significantly above or below the standard normally expected for his or her age, another book may be more appropriate. If you are not sure which to choose, two simple **Entry tests** are available to help you identify the book that is best suited to the pupil's abilities. You can also use these resources with new pupils joining your class or school.

Photocopy masters of the **Entry tests** are provided in the teacher's guide – which also contains the **Entry test marking keys**, full instructions for use, and a range of other **English Skills** copymasters, including **Diagnostic checks**, which help to identify topics that pupils may be struggling with. The **Diagnostic check marking keys** provide catch-up activities for each topic, in the form of activity prompts, to help secure pupils' knowledge. For ordering details, see page 46.

You may be using **English Skills** at Key Stage 3 or with other mixed-ability groups of young people or adults. In such cases you will find the **Entry tests** vital in deciding which book to give each student.

Published by **Schofield & Sims Ltd**, 7 Mariner Court, Wakefield, West Yorkshire WF4 3FL, UK
Telephone 01484 607080
www.schofieldandsims.co.uk

First edition published in 2011
This edition copyright © Schofield & Sims Ltd, 2017
Third impression 2021

Author: **Carol Matchett**
Carol Matchett has asserted her moral right under the Copyright, Designs and Patents Act, 1988, to be identified as the author of this work.

British Library Cataloguing in Publication Data
A catalogue record for this book is available from the British Library.

Design by **Ledgard Jepson Ltd**
Front cover design by **Peter Grundy**
Printed in the UK by **Page Bros (Norwich) Ltd**

ISBN 978 07217 1411 0

CONTENTS

Introduction

Schofield & Sims English Skills provides regular and carefully graded practice in key literacy skills. It is designed for use alongside your existing English lessons, embedding key aspects of grammar, sentence structure, punctuation and spelling and constantly revisiting them until they become automatic. At the same time, it reinforces and develops pupils' knowledge of word structure and vocabulary.

Each pupil book comprises three sections with 12 tests in each one. The tests become more difficult, but the increase in difficulty is gradual. The pupil books are fully compatible with the Key Stage 2 National Curriculum, and the final tests in each book are aligned with the end-of-year objectives as follows:

- **Introductory Book:** Years 1 and 2 (Bridge to lower KS2)
- **Book 1:** Year 3
- **Book 2:** Year 4
- **Book 3:** Years 4 and 5 (Bridge to upper KS2)
- **Book 4:** Year 5
- **Book 5:** Year 6
- **Book 6:** Years 6 and 7 (Bridge to KS3)

Parts A, B and C

Each test is divided into three parts:

- Part A: **Warm-up** – puzzles, 'warm-up' exercises and revision of earlier learning
- Part B: **Word work** – spelling, word structure, exploring words and their meanings to help develop vocabulary
- Part C: **Sentence work** – constructing and punctuating sentences; using words from different word classes; understanding tense, verb forms and other aspects of grammar.

Answering the test questions

After you have demonstrated to the class how some of the different question types are to be answered, the pupils work through the test items without adult help – either individually or in pairs. Encourage them to refer to dictionaries, thesauruses and other appropriate reference materials rather than asking for your help. The tests may be used flexibly. For example, a test may be tackled in one session or over several days.

Marking

This book provides correct answers for **English Skills 4**; where various different answers would be acceptable, an example is provided. The **Focus** panel stating the areas of learning being tested helps you to decide whether the pupil's answer is satisfactory. **Please note and explain to the class that if all or part of a question has several possible answers, the question number is displayed like this ⑤. If a question has a specific answer, the question number is displayed like this ❺. It is displayed in this way even if the answer is made up of several parts that may be given in any order.**

Some questions test more than one area: for example, a question on writing in the past tense might also check pupils' knowledge of the spelling rules for adding **ed**. In such cases, both parts of the answer must be correct, reflecting real-life situations that require varied knowledge and skills.

Group marking sessions

Some teachers find that group or class marking sessions led by the teacher or classroom assistant are the most effective way of marking the tests: pupils learn by comparing and discussing answers.

Another benefit of group or class marking sessions is that they quickly highlight gaps in pupils' knowledge, which will help to inform your future teaching. Where pupils have given a wrong answer, or none at all, briefly reinforce the key teaching point using an item from this book as a model. At the end of the session, encourage pupils to evaluate their own successes and identify what they need to remember next time or when they are writing.

Suggested questions to ask in a marking session:
- What was this question testing?
- How many different 'correct' answers did we come up with?
- Were some sentence or word choices more interesting or effective than others? Why?
- How do we know this answer is correct?
- How can we make the answer correct?
- Is there an answer that would be even better?
- What are the key points to remember next time?
- When might we put these key points into practice in our reading or writing?

Marking the end-of-section assessments

At the end of each section are two writing assessments: the **Writing task** and the **Proofreading task**. These check that pupils are applying in their writing the knowledge, skills and understanding developed in the weekly tests. The assessments also provide evidence of a pupil's strengths and weaknesses, which will help you to set appropriate targets. You might consider sharing with the pupils a simplified version of the mark scheme – and then involve them in setting their own targets for improving their writing.

• *The writing task*

The **Writing task** helps you assess a pupil's written composition. Prompts help pupils to plan and gather ideas so that when they begin writing they can focus on selecting appropriate grammar, vocabulary and sentence structures to express their ideas clearly and effectively. On pages 16, 30 and 44 you will find photocopiable **Writing task assessment sheets** – one for each section – with specific assessment points arranged under the headings 'Sentence structure and punctuation', 'Composition and effect' and 'Spelling'. Complete one of these sheets as you mark each pupil's work.

• *The proofreading task*

The **Proofreading task** focuses on correcting punctuation, grammar and spelling. Examples of **Completed proofreading tasks** for each section, also photocopiable, are supplied on pages 17, 31 and 45. However, please note that pupils may choose to correct some of the errors using methods different to those shown in the example, but which are equally valid. For example, two main clauses might be joined using a conjunction or separated to make two sentences. Additional evidence gained from the relevant **Proofreading task** will help you to further assess pupils' achievements in 'Sentence punctuation' and 'Spelling' as already assessed in the **Writing task**. If you wish, you can use the photocopiable sheet to make notes on a pupil's work.

Please note: Where the assessment statements reveal weaknesses in a pupil's writing, work with the pupil to identify areas to develop and set targets for future writing. All the books revisit difficult areas so there will also be more opportunities for further practice.

Progress chart

On page 46 of the pupil book you will find a **Progress chart**, with one column each for Sections 1, 2 and 3, and a list of 'I can' statements relating to the kinds of activities practised in the section. Please ask every pupil to complete the relevant column when they have finished working through a section.

The **Progress chart** encourages pupils to monitor their own work by identifying those activities that they have mastered and those requiring further attention. When pupils colour in the chart as recommended (green for easy, orange for getting there and red for difficult), it gives a clear picture of progress. It also shows the benefits of systematic practice: an activity that the pupil cannot perform in Section 1 later gets the 'green light'.

The **Progress chart** promotes self-assessment and personalised learning. However, you may also wish to make a copy for your own record-keeping. For this reason, it may be photocopied.

SECTION 1 | Test 1

A Warm-up

Add an adverb.

1. She spoke _hesitantly_ about her feelings.
2. He was _severely_ punished for the crime.
3. _Casually,_ they walked off down the road.

Add the same missing consonants to each of the three words.

4. s t o m a **c h**   m o n a r **c h**   **c h** a s m
5. a **s** c e n t   m u **s** c l e   d e **s** c e n d

Put the letters in order to make a word.

6. **e g s s u**   _guess_
7. **a g v u e**   _vague_
8. **e q u i n u**   _unique_

Add the same prefix to each set of words.

9. _al_ most   _al_ though   _al_ mighty
10. _ex_ change   _ex_ claim   _ex_ tend

B Word work

Underline the prefix and suffix/es. Write the root word.

1. <u>dis</u>approv<u>ingly</u>   _approve_
2. <u>dis</u>solv<u>ing</u>   _solve_

Add **ous** to change the word into an adjective.

3. **victory**   _victorious_
4. **adventure**   _adventurous_
5. **marvel**   _marvellous_
6. **mischief**   _mischievous_

Sort the words into two groups.

frustrated livid irritated enraged

7. **very angry**   _livid, enraged_
8. **quite angry**   _frustrated, irritated_

Add two synonyms to each group.

9. **very happy**   _ecstatic, overjoyed_
10. **quite happy**   _pleased, content_

C Sentence work

Complete the sentence with a subordinate clause.

1. After _everyone had calmed down,_ we had a great time.
2. While _the sun was shining,_ we had a great time.
3. Although _the campsite was disappointing,_ we had a great time.
4. Before _the rain came,_ we had a great time.

Complete the sentence by adding at least two adverbials that add further detail.

5. The young man sang _happily to himself as he walked along the road._
6. Ellie gazed _wistfully out of the window at the crowded city below._
7. The little dog looked _at him sadly with his big brown eyes._
8. The women looked _in amazement around the bare empty room._

It was beginning to rain, big heavy drops fell from the sky, the picnic was over.

9. What is wrong with the punctuation? _Commas are used where stronger punctuation is needed._
10. Write it correctly.

   It was beginning to rain. Big heavy drops fell from the sky. The picnic was over.

X DEFINITIVE ANSWER   X SAMPLE ANSWER

A Warm-up

Complete the simile using a suitable noun phrase.

1. mad as *a troop of monkeys*

2. cheerful as *a laughing hyena*

3. lazy as *a sloth up a tree*

4. greedy as *a guzzling goat*

Add the missing suffix to complete the word.

5. occasion *al* ly

6. worth *less* ness

7. except *ion* al

PART A Focus
1–4: similes; noun phrases
5–7: word structure
8–10: spelling strategies

Write a word that contains these letters. The letters must be used in this order.

8. **h g t** *height*

9. **p s b** *possible*

10. **m n t** *minute*

B Word work

Write in the missing letter string.

1. w *eigh* t l e s s n e s s

2. n *eigh* b o u r

PART B Focus
1–2: letter string eigh
3–7: homophones and words that are often confused
8–10: meaning of common roots

Underline the correct word of the two that appear in brackets.

3. I ate my (desert / <u>dessert</u>).

4. How did you know? *Because dessert is the one you eat.*

5. I always watch this (cereal / <u>serial</u>) on TV.

6. How did you know? *Because a serial is a series of programmes (you eat cereal).*

7. Write the homophone.

    morning *mourning*   **seen** *scene*

All three words come from the same root. Underline the root.

8. <u>therm</u>al <u>therm</u>ometer <u>therm</u>ostat

9. <u>aqua</u>rium <u>aqua</u>tic <u>Aqua</u>rius

What do the root words mean?

10. *therm* = *heat*   *aqua* = *water*

C Sentence work

Turn each sentence into a question (Q) and a command (C).

1. Let's go to the cinema.
   Q: *Shall we go to the cinema?*
   C: *Go to the cinema.*

2. You could bake a cake.
   Q: *Would you like to bake a cake?*
   C: *Bake a cake.*

3. We could form two teams.
   Q: *Shall we form two teams?*
   C: *Form two teams.*

Add adjectives to create the given mood.

4. **calm, peaceful**   The *soft* moonlight gave a *delicate* glow to the *whispering* trees.

5. **threatening, sinister** The *pale* moonlight gave an *eerie* glow to the *shadowy* trees.

6. Which three determiners are used in sentences 4 and 5? *the* *a* *an*

PART C Focus
1–3: questions and commands
4–5: adjectives; selecting vocabulary for effect
6: word classes: determiners
7–10: apostrophes for possession

Rewrite the phrase using three words and a possessive apostrophe.

7. the instruments belonging to the band   *the band's instruments*

8. the party held for the three brothers   *the brothers' party*

9. the club belonging to the supporters   *the supporters' club*

10. the staffroom for the teachers   *the teachers' staffroom*

X DEFINITIVE ANSWER   X SAMPLE ANSWER

A Warm-up

lion sandwich

1. Write a statement using these words.

    A lion stole my sandwich.

2. Write a question using these words.

    Did a lion really steal your sandwich?

Add the missing vowels.
You may use a letter twice if necessary.

PART A Focus
1–2: forming statements and questions
3–6: spelling patterns
7–10: meaning of prefixes

a e u

3. b e a u t y

4. a u t u m n

5. r e s t a u r a n t

6. f a u l t y

7. These words and prefixes are mixed up.
    Write them correctly.

    minisecond **micro**bus **nano**chip

    minibus, microchip, nanosecond

8. What do the word roots have in common?

    They are all to do with smallness.

Write two more words with the prefix shown in **bold**.

9. **mini**   minimum, miniature

10. **micro**   microphone, microscope

B Word work

Write in the missing pronoun.

I can do it myself.

PART B Focus
1–3: reflexive pronouns; plural spellings
4–6: building words from root words
7–10: figures of speech

1. She can do it   herself   .

2. We can do it   ourselves   .

3. They can do it   themselves   .

Write three words formed from the root word **press**.

4. impress

5. depressingly

6. pressure

Write the meaning of the phrase.

7. **to turn over a new leaf**

    to make a fresh start

8. **to feel under the weather**

    to feel unwell

9. **That rings a bell!**

    That sounds familiar!

10. What do you notice about these phrases?

    They are not meant to be taken literally.

C Sentence work

Continue the sentence, to explain or give a reason. Use a preposition or conjunction.

1. **People are uneasy** about the future of the project.

2. **Josh rushed through the door** to show his mother the letter.

3. **Fold the paper in half** so that you make a triangle shape.

4. **The boy watched the cat** as it climbed up into the tree.

Underline the pronouns in the sentence.

5. **Rosie and Jess were supposed to share the biscuits but she kept them for herself.**

6. Why is the sentence confusing? Because 'she' could mean Rosie or Jess kept them.

Write the sentence so the meaning is clear.

7. Although she was supposed to share the biscuits with Jess, Rosie kept them for herself.

Write the dialogue correctly.

PART C Focus
1–4: extending sentences; using prepositions and conjunctions to give reasons
5–7: checking accurate use of pronouns; ambiguity
8–10: punctuating direct speech

8. **We must leave said David.**   "We must leave," said David.

9. **When asked Anna.**   "When?" asked Anna.

10. **Very soon David replied.**   "Very soon," David replied.

 ⊗ DEFINITIVE ANSWER   ⊗ SAMPLE ANSWER

A Warm-up

Add the correct word endings.

1. The rain fell heavy _ily_ , leave _ing_ a lay _er_ of moist _ure_ on the grass.

2. Luck _ily_ , the drive _r_ kept his compose _ure_ and avoid _ed_ two lorry _ies_ .

Complete the word sum.

3. **occupy + ing** = _occupying_

4. **occupy + ation** = _occupation_

5. **occupy + er** = _occupier_

> **PART A Focus**
> **1–5:** rules for adding word endings
> **6:** homophones
> **7–10:** using prepositions

6. Write the homophone.

threw _through_   **heard** _herd_

Add a phrase starting with a preposition.

across before through to

7. The tiger prowled _through the forest._

8. The swans swam _across the river._

9. The turtle spoke _to the monkey._

10. The lion arrived _before breakfast._

B Word work

The same letter string is missing from all these words. Write it in.

1. e n _ough_   a l t h _ough_

2. t h r _ough_   b r _ough_ t

3. What do you notice? _The letter string can make different sounds._

4. Write two more words with this letter string.

cough, bough

Draw a line to join the word to another word from the same family.

> **PART B Focus**
> **1–4:** common letter strings with different sounds
> **5–9:** word roots and word families
> **10:** adverbs with similar meanings

5. noun ———— anniversary
6. voice ———— announce
7. annual ———— vocal

Write two words formed from the root.

8. **graph** _graphic, autograph_

9. **circum** _circumference, circumstance_

10. Underline the synonyms of **sadly**.

politely <u>dejectedly</u> gleefully <u>dismally</u>

C Sentence work

Complete the simile with a descriptive noun phrase.

1. A still pond is like _a mirror to the sky._

2. Autumn leaves are like _shimmering butterflies._

3. A volcano is like _a fire-breathing dragon._

4. A poppy is like _red tissue paper._

Cross out some words and phrases and write new ones that make the performance sound more impressive.

5. Cleaver ~~sent a good~~ high ball into the penalty area and Jones ~~got it into the net~~.

lofted, terrific, rose to head it home

6. The goalkeeper ~~jumped well~~ and ~~knocked~~ the ball just over the crossbar.

leapt agilely, tipped

7. After some ~~good~~ play from Cleaver, Robinson ~~sent a good~~ ball past the stranded keeper.

brilliant, curved a masterful

> **PART C Focus**
> **1–4:** using descriptive noun phrases; similes
> **5–7:** selecting vocabulary for effect
> **8–10:** using commas after fronted adverbials

Add the missing commas.

8. Although it was dark, I knew someone was following me.

9. Before we begin, let's check everyone is here.

10. Completely exhausted, the two children soon fell fast asleep.

X DEFINITIVE ANSWER   X SAMPLE ANSWER

A Warm-up

Complete the sentence.

1. Sam made tea. Meanwhile, _Jon sat by the fire and read the paper._

2. Sam made tea. Suddenly, _a crashing sound came from the living room._

3. Sam made tea. Afterwards, _they all sat at the table to drink it._

Add the same three letters to all three words.

4. ear **t h**   w **ear** y   h **ear** d

5. c e r t **ain**   b a r g **ain**   f o u n t **ain**

6. v a p **our**   h o n **our**   n **our** i s h

7. Underline the word that is **not** a real word.

   artist novelist <u>photographist</u> stockist

Write three more words ending with **ist**.

8. scientist

9. dentist

10. specialist

PART A Focus
1–3: adverbs to link ideas or events
4–6: letter strings
7–10: suffixes: ist

B Word work

Add **ible** or **able**.

1. suit _able_   enjoy _able_   fashion _able_

2. terr _ible_   ed _ible_   horr _ible_

3. How are the **able** words different from the **ible** words?

   'Able' is added when there is already a whole word there.

PART B Focus
1–3: spelling patterns: able, ible
4–6: prefixes: in, im, il, ir
7: letter string augh
8–10: meaning of adverbs; inferring meaning from word structure

Add the correct prefix.

il   in   im   ir

4. _il_ legible   _ir_ reversible

5. _in_ capable   _im_ probable

6. How do the prefixes change the word?

   They make the opposite meaning.

7. Add the same letter string to all three words.

   c _augh_ t   l _augh_ t e r   d i s t r _augh_ t

Write a definition.

8. **disapprovingly**   _as if you don't approve_

9. **enthusiastically**   _excitedly_

10. **courteously**   _politely_

C Sentence work

Rewrite the sentence so that it begins with the adverbial.

1. The tent collapsed as I stood up.   _As I stood up, the tent collapsed._

2. The room was strangely silent.   _Strangely, the room was silent._

3. There was a faint rumble from far away.   _From far away, there was a faint rumble._

Underline the word that makes the meaning of the sentence unclear.

4. The dog watched the cat carefully as <u>it</u> sat under the tree.

5. Oliver ignored Luke as <u>he</u> walked down the corridor.

Give a reason for each of your answers.

6. _Because 'it' could be the dog or the cat._

7. _Because 'he' could be Oliver or Luke._

What punctuation mark is hidden by the symbol?

8. Thank you for the present ▲ Robbie. What a lovely surprise ♠

   ▲ is _a comma_   ♠ is _an exclamation mark_

9. You will come and visit us ▲ won't you ● Yes ▲ I'll come next week.

   ▲ is _a comma_   ● is _a question mark_

10. The little girl ♦ Sally) was only five years old ▼ Dylan was ten.

   ♦ is _a bracket_   ▼ is _a full stop_

PART C Focus
1–3: reordering sentences; fronted adverbials
4–7: accurate use of pronouns
8–10: use of commas and brackets; sentence punctuation

X DEFINITIVE ANSWER   X SAMPLE ANSWER

A Warm-up

Write three sentences using these words only.

waited they nervously

(1) They waited nervously.

(2) Nervously, they waited.

(3) They nervously waited.

(4) Add the **ing** ending.

spiral ling   crackle ing   marvel ling

Draw a line to join the word to a suffix and make a new noun.

(5) free ⎯⎯⎯ ship
(6) false ⎯⎯⎯ hood
(7) partner ⎯⎯⎯ dom

Write the noun as a plural.

(8) **battery**   batteries
(9) **library**   libraries
(10) **piano**   pianos

PART A Focus
1–3: word order; moving adverbs
4: rules for adding verb endings
5–7: suffixes
8–10: plural spelling rules

B Word work

Add the missing vowels.

(1) d e t e r m i n e d
(2) d e s p e r a t e
(3) d e f i n i t e
(4) d i f f e r e n t

PART B Focus
1–4: unstressed vowels; words that are often misspelt
5–6: suffixes: ation
7–10: forming and using nouns ending tion

(5) Add the suffix **ation** to make a noun.

converse ation   tempt ation   expect ation

(6) Add **ation** to the verb to make a noun. Write the new word. Check the spelling.

exclaim   exclamation

explain   explanation

Complete the sentence with a noun formed from one of these root words.

consume irrigate pollute pure

(7) Factory waste can cause water pollution .

(8) Purification makes water safe to drink.

(9) Irrigation is vital for crops to grow.

(10) Find ways to cut water consumption .

C Sentence work

(1) Write eight verbs that would be suitable to fill the gap.

Alfie _____ come home.

has, might, could, will, may, had, should, must

(2) Write two verbs that would make the perfect verb form.   had, has

(3) Write two verbs that could refer to future events.   might, will

Write two adverbs that give different views of the character.

(4) "What are you doing?" asked the boy   politely / sharply .

(5) "Come on then," said Maria   cheerfully / gloomily .

(6) "I'll take that," the woman said   greedily / helpfully .

Cross out the incorrect words in the sentence.

(7) Many **animals** ~~animal's animals'~~ have made this their home.

(8) There are two doctors. This is the ~~doctors doctor's~~ **doctors'** surgery.

(9) That is the home ~~teams~~ **team's** ~~teams'~~ dressing room.

(10) That is the ~~childrens~~ **children's** ~~childrens'~~ playground.

PART C Focus
1–3: verb forms
4–6: choosing adverbs for effect
7–10: apostrophe for possession; plural s and possessive s

(X) DEFINITIVE ANSWER   (X) SAMPLE ANSWER

A Warm-up

Rewrite the sentence, adding a subordinate clause.

1 **He stood up.** He stood up when the teacher entered the room.

2 **Someone screamed.** As the lights went out, someone screamed.

3 **They won.** They won because they were the better team.

Add the same prefix to all three words.

4 *de* code   *de* form   *de* flate

5 *re* place   *re* move   *re* view

6 *mis* take   *mis* count   *mis* lead

Write in the missing word.

it's its

7 It's great here!

8 The dog buried its bone.

9 The tree shook its leaves.

10 I hope it's not too late.

> **PART A Focus**
> **1–3:** subordinate clauses
> **4–6:** prefixes
> **7–10:** using it's and its

B Word work

Add the correct plural ending.

1 photo s   radio s

2 potato es   hero es

> **PART B Focus**
> **1–2:** plurals of words ending with o
> **3–4:** words that are often confused
> **5–8:** prefixes
> **9–10:** word roots

3 Add the missing letters.

s c

d e c e n t   d e s c e n t   d i s s e n t

4 Use two of the words in these sentences.

It was a decent attempt.

It was a difficult descent from Everest.

These words and prefixes are mixed up.
Write them correctly.

sublight **uni**merge **micro**natural **super**form

5 submerge

6 microlight

7 uniform

8 supernatural

Write three words that use the root word.

9 **verb (meaning word)**

verbose, verbal, adverb

10 **cent (meaning one hundred)**

century, percentage, centigrade

C Sentence work

Write three sentences using the words **thieves** and **boxes**.

1 with one clause   The thieves stole several boxes of clothing.

2 using **but**   Thieves broke into a warehouse but took only empty boxes.

3 starting with a conjunction   As the thieves fled, they dropped the boxes.

Complete the phrase and add apostrophes to show which of these groups owns what.

the driver the bakers the crew the horses

> **PART C Focus**
> **1–3:** varying sentences and clauses
> **4–7:** possessive apostrophes
> **8–9:** selecting vocabulary for effect
> **10:** noun phrases

4 the bakers' oven

5 the driver's van

6 the horses' stables

7 the crew's spaceship

Complete the sentence, choosing words for effect.

8 The man plunged into the woods, branches cracking under his feet, the beast clawing at his coat.

9 He saw its fearsome eyes were round like saucers . He smelt its filthy coat of matted fur.

10 Write the noun phrase from above that includes a determiner, adjective and preposition phrase.

its filthy coat of matted fur

X DEFINITIVE ANSWER   X SAMPLE ANSWER

A Warm-up

Add adverbs to show **when** and **where**.

1 The fire engine _soon_ arrived _outside_ .

2 _Later_ he fell asleep _upstairs_ .

Complete the three adjectives.

3 a w e _some_

4 a w _ful_

5 a w k _ward_

> **PART A Focus**
> 1–2: adverbs to show time and place
> 3–7: words that are often misspelt
> 8–10: similes; descriptive noun phrases

Add the missing letters. **Clue:** *fractions*

6 e _i_ g h t h   t w e _l_ _f_ t h

7 n _i_ n t h   h u n d _r_ e d t h

The flob is an imaginary creature. Add a noun phrase to complete these similes describing it.

8 It moves like _a giant green caterpillar._

9 It sounds like _a squelching jelly._

10 It eats like _a vacuum cleaner._

B Word work

Add the missing letters.

1 i n c r e d _i_ b l e   3 r e m a r k _a_ b l e

2 v i s _i_ b l e   4 r e a s o n _a_ b l e

Add a prefix and a suffix to make a new word.

5 _ir_ resist _ible_   **Clue:** *very tempting*

6 _im_ prison _ed_   **Clue:** *locked up*

7 _in_ effect _ive_   **Clue:** *useless*

> **PART B Focus**
> 1–4: able and ible
> 5–7: word structure
> 8–10: figures of speech

Complete the well-known saying and write a definition.

8 you can't judge a book by _its cover_

   means _don't make judgements based_

   on appearances

9 got out of bed on _the wrong side_

   means _in a bad mood_

10 over the _moon_

   means _very pleased_

C Sentence work

Write a sentence to follow the headline. Use adverbials to include details about the events.

1 Class G takes the plunge!   _On Friday, Class G at Welford Primary School braved the chilly weather with a sponsored swim at their school._

2 School concert raises the roof!   _A concert on Tuesday by pupils at Welford Primary School received enthusiastic applause._

3 Bookbusters are go!   _The first meeting of a new after-school book club was held on Monday in the library._

Draw a line to show the verb form used in the sentence.

4 Ben and Angie were late.——————→ present progressive

5 No-one has seen them.——————→ past tense

6 Aunt Lucy is waiting for them.——————→ perfect form

> **PART C Focus**
> 1–3: using adverbials to add details about time and place
> 4–6: verb forms
> 7–10: punctuating direct speech

Rewrite the sentence as direct speech.

7 Eve asked Ross if he was OK.   _"Are you OK, Ross?" asked Eve._

8 Mohammed said his house was ruined.   _"My house is ruined," said Mohammed._

9 The genie told him the magic word (yoyo).   _"The magic word is 'yoyo'," said the genie._

10 Lucy asked for the shoes in her size (size 2).   _"Do you have these shoes in size 2?" asked Lucy._

X DEFINITIVE ANSWER   X SAMPLE ANSWER

A Warm-up

Continue the sentence after the conjunction.

1 Terry was anxious in case _someone had_
   seen him.

2 Terry was anxious even though _he was_
   well prepared.

3 Terry was anxious whenever _he was_
   left alone in the house.

4 Terry was anxious until _Sam arrived._

PART A Focus
1–4: using a range of conjunctions
5–7: word roots
8–10: spelling rules and patterns

Write two words with this root.

5 **tri** (means 3)   _triangle, triathlon_

6 **octo** (means 8)   _octagon, octopus_

7 **dec** (means 10)   _decimal, decade_

Cross out the word that is wrongly spelt.
Write the correct spelling.

8 special social ~~parcial~~   _partial_

9 curious ~~hidious~~ previous   _hideous_

10 reliable ~~edable~~ available   _edible_

B Word work

Add the missing letters.

1 f r i g h t e n i n g

2 t e m p e r a t u r e

3 a v e r a g e

4 g e n e r a l l y

PART B Focus
1–4: unstressed vowels; words that are often misspelt
5: words ending tion, sion
6: spelling patterns: gu
7–10: root words; word structure

5 Add the ending that sounds like 'shun'.
   Write the new word.

promote	_promotion_
discuss	_discussion_
erode	_erosion_
illustrate	_illustration_

6 Add the same missing letters to all three words.
   g u a r d   g u a r a n t e e   l a n g u a g e

Write three words formed from the root word.

7 **child**   _children, childhood, childlike_

8 **pain**   _painful, painless, painstaking_

9 **hand**   _handle, handler, handkerchief_

10 **move**   _moveable, movie, remove_

C Sentence work

Draw a line to show how the underlined words are used in the sentence.

1 Bake <u>until the top is golden.</u>   — preposition phrase

2 Select the text <u>with the highlighter.</u>   — adverb

3 <u>Then</u> cut <u>carefully</u> along the dotted line.   — subordinate clause

PART C Focus
1–6: using prepositions, conjunctions and adverbs to show how, where and when
7–10: fronted adverbials; commas after fronted adverbials

Complete the sentences about words used in questions 1–3.

4 The conjunction _until_ is used in sentence _1_ to _show how much time to bake it for_ .

5 The adverbs _then_ and _carefully_ are used in sentence _3_ to _say when and how to cut it_ .

6 The prepositions _with_ and _along_ are used in sentences _2_ and _3_ .

Reorder the sentence so that it starts with an adverbial. Punctuate the sentence correctly.

7 The door opened easily, much to his surprise. _Much to his surprise, the door opened easily._

8 Jack ran out of the door, grabbing the golden egg.
   Grabbing the golden egg, Jack ran out of the door.

9 A light shone faintly from far away. _From far away, a light shone faintly._

10 Amy forgot her worries for a while huddled by the fire.
   Huddled by the fire, Amy forgot her worries for a while.

X DEFINITIVE ANSWER   X SAMPLE ANSWER

A Warm-up

Complete the sentence.

1. Gradually, *the mist lifted.*
2. Surprisingly, *the room was empty.*
3. Determinedly, *he began to climb.*

4. Write a sentence using the word **clear** as a verb and an adjective.

   verb *We need to clear the table.*

   adjective *The water was clear.*

5. Write the correct spelling.

   croose *cruise*   pursoot *pursuit*

   broose *bruise*   noosance *nuisance*

Add the missing vowels to the plural nouns.

Clue: musical instruments

6. b a n j o s
7. c e l l o s
8. p i c c o l o s
9. b o n g o s
10. p i a n o s

> **PART A Focus**
> **1–3:** using fronted adverbials
> **4:** word classes
> **5:** spelling patterns
> **6–10:** plural spelling of words ending with o

B Word work

Add the missing letters.

1. s e v e r a l
2. r e l e v a n t

Cross out the words that are wrong. Write the correct spellings.

> **PART B Focus**
> **1–2:** unstressed vowels in words that are often misspelt
> **3–5:** checking for spelling errors; homophones
> **6–10:** word roots; meanings

3. ~~Led~~ and ~~steal~~ are metals.

   lead   *steel*

4. I felt a cold ~~draft~~.   *draught*

5. I ~~guest~~ the ~~whether mite altar~~ your plans.

   guessed   *weather*   *might*   *alter*

6. Write four words using these roots and prefixes only.

   auto para graph chute photo

   autograph, paragraph,
   photograph, parachute

Use the same roots to make two words that do **not** exist.

7. *autochute*   8. *paraphoto*

Write the meaning of the root word.

9. **graph** *to write*   10. **photo** *light*

C Sentence work

Rewrite this sentence using different verb forms.

Shadows creep across the lawn.

1. **past tense** *Shadows crept across the lawn.*
2. **past progressive** *Shadows were creeping across the lawn.*
3. **present perfect form** *Shadows have crept across the lawn.*

Write three words that would sound correct if used to fill the gap.

4. We had pizza _____ the film.   *before, after, during*
5. Unfortunately, _____ children were late.   *some, the, two*

6. Underline what type of word you have written.

   In Q4: adverbs conjunctions <u>prepositions</u>   In Q5: <u>determiners</u> nouns pronouns

Use brackets to add an extra comment or piece of information.

7. Auntie Agnes is coming on Saturday (*worst luck*).
8. My name is Richard (*Ricky to my friends*) and I am ten.
9. We had lasagna (*my favourite*) for tea.
10. Raj (*who is my cousin*) came to stay.

> **PART C Focus**
> **1–3:** verb forms; progressive and perfect
> **4–6:** word classes
> **7–10:** using brackets

X DEFINITIVE ANSWER   X SAMPLE ANSWER

A Warm-up

Use the word **kitten** in each of the following.

1. **a sentence** — The kitten played with the ball.

2. **an exclamation** — What a lovely kitten!

3. **a question** — Have you seen my kitten?

4. **a command** — Leave the kitten alone.

Write three verbs to use in place of

5. **likes** — loves, adores, appreciates

6. **dislikes** — hates, loathes, despises

Add the missing letters.

Clue: useful in snow

7. s n o w p l ough
8. b o b s l eigh
9. t o b o ggan
10. s n o w b oard

PART A Focus
1–4: sentence types
5–6: synonyms
7–10: spelling patterns

B Word work

Underline the two correct spellings.

1. regreting <u>regretted</u> regretible <u>regrettable</u>
2. <u>limited</u> limitting <u>limitation</u> limittation

PART B Focus
1–2: rules for adding suffixes
3–6: rules for adding able
7–10: prefixes; inferring meaning from word structure

Add the suffix **able**.

3. **rely** — reliable   **envy** — enviable
4. **value** — valuable   **adore** — adorable

What two spelling rules did you use?

5. Change the 'y' to an 'i' to add 'able'.
6. Drop the final 'e' to add 'able'.

The prefix **mal** means **bad** or **badly**.
Use this information to define these words.

7. **malfunction** — breaks down or works badly
8. **malware** — bad or harmful software

The prefix **trans** means **across**.
Use this information to define these words.

9. **transatlantic** — across the Atlantic
10. **transplant** — to take from one place and move across to somewhere else

C Sentence work

Is this a simile or a metaphor? Write your answer.

PART C Focus
1–4: similes and metaphors
5–6: noun phrases for description
7–9: punctuating speech; direct and reported speech
10: using subordinating conjunctions

1. Clouds are like cotton wool.   simile
2. Clouds of cotton wool float in the sky.   metaphor

Write a simile and a metaphor about snowflakes.

3. **simile** — Snowflakes fall like blossom.
4. **metaphor** — Snowflakes are winter blossom in the frozen sky.

Expand the noun into a longer, descriptive noun phrase.

5. a quaint little **cottage** with roses round the door
6. a huge **lake** of clear blue water

7. Add the punctuation to the dialogue.

    Zoë: Have you seen this film, Jack?

    Jack: No, I haven't.

8. Write the dialogue as direct speech.

    "Have you seen this film, Jack?" asked Zoë.

    "No, I haven't," replied Jack.

9. Write the dialogue as reported speech. Zoë asked Jack if he had seen the film, but he hadn't.

10. Write a sentence using the words **girl**, **rabbit** and **although**.

    The girl thought she had seen the rabbit, although she wasn't sure.

X DEFINITIVE ANSWER   X SAMPLE ANSWER

A Warm-up

Write a simile to describe

1. **grass** like a rug flung over the garden

2. **a spider's web** like spokes on a wheel

3. **lightning** like a crack in the sky

4. Underline the word that you **cannot** add **able** to.

   drink port bend <u>water</u> work

Add a prefix and a suffix to make a new word.

5. re place ment   *Clue: substitute*

6. de sign er   *Clue: someone who designs*

7. in expense ive   *Clue: cheap*

Add a letter to the middle of the word to make another word. Write the new word.

8. **though**   through

9. **wary**   weary

10. **county**   country

> **PART A Focus**
> **1–3:** descriptive noun phrases
> **4–7:** word structure
> **8–10:** spelling patterns

B Word work

Add the suffix **ation**.

1. **admire**   admiration

2. **vary**   variation

Add **able** to the words to form adjectives.

3. **admire**   admirable

4. **vary**   variable

Imagine that the word in **bold** really existed. What would it mean?

5. **subvision**   seeing under things

6. **supership**   a very large ship

Write a definition of these compound words, found in a computer manual.

7. **desktop** the workspace on a computer screen

8. **download** to copy files onto a computer

9. **interface** the link between the user and the computer

10. **firewall** protection for a computer

> **PART B Focus**
> **1–4:** adding ation and able
> **5–6:** meaning of prefixes; word meanings
> **7–10:** subject-specific word meanings

C Sentence work

Rewrite these statements in Standard English.

1. It felt real exciting seeing in the paper the picture what I drew.

   It felt really exciting seeing in the paper the picture that I had drawn.

2. I seen her eating them cakes what you brought.

   I saw her eating those cakes that you brought.

3. They was there. I seen them with me own eyes. They were there. I saw them with my own eyes.

4. I didn't say nothing to no-one. I didn't say anything to anyone.

5. Write a metaphor to describe a sunset.   **The sky has been** washed with orange paint.

Put a tick if the punctuation is correct. Put a cross if it is not.

6. "Dont drink that" screamed Josie. "Its Jakes magic potion."   ✗

7. He stood still. He listened. Not a sound could be heard.   ✓

8. The room was empty, there was no carpet on the floor.   ✗

> **PART C Focus**
> **1–4:** Standard English
> **5:** writing metaphors
> **6–10:** checking punctuation

Write the incorrect sentences correctly.

9. "Don't drink that!" screamed Josie. "It's Jake's magic potion!"

10. The room was empty. There was no carpet on the floor.

Remind the pupil to complete Section 1 of the Progress chart on page 46 of the pupil book.

Ⓧ DEFINITIVE ANSWER   Ⓧ SAMPLE ANSWER

Writing task assessment sheet: Jam sandwich!

Name: _____ Class/Set: _____

Teacher's name: _____ Date: _____

Sentence structure and punctuation

	Always/often	Sometimes	Never
A range of conjunctions is used to write sentences with more than one clause (e.g. **while**, **after**, **although**)			
Sentences are extended using adverbials (adverbs, prepositions, conjunctions)			
Sentence construction is varied for effect (e.g. fronted adverbials)			
Expanded noun phrases are used to add detail			
Standard English is used in news report			
Appropriate use of tense (including progressive and perfect forms)			
Sentences are demarcated accurately (no comma splice)			
Capital letters are used for names			
Commas are used correctly in sentences (lists, fronted adverbials)			
Direct speech is punctuated correctly			
Apostrophes are used for contractions and possession			
Some use of other punctuation (e.g. brackets)			

Composition and effect

Features of a newspaper are used (e.g. headline, opening sentence, use of quotes)			
Paragraphs are used to develop ideas			
Ideas are selected to inform/engage			
Adverbials are used to show shifts in time, place and focus			
Language is chosen for effect (e.g. headlines)			
Appropriate tone and language are used for newspaper report			

Spelling

Knowledge of spelling patterns is applied correctly			
Longer words are correct, including suffixes and endings (e.g. **ous**, **able**, **ible**)			
Correct spelling of words that are often misspelt (e.g. words with unstressed vowels)			
Rules for adding prefixes are applied correctly			
Rules for adding verb endings and suffixes are applied correctly			
Spelling of plurals is correct			
Correct choice of homophones			

Completed proofreading task: Ricky the runner

Name: _____   Class/Set: _____

Teacher's name: _____   Date: _____

Let me tell you about my bruther [o] Ricky. He's [,] eight years old, has spikey [,] hair like a spider plant and a mischievus [o] smile. some [S] people think he is cute but actually [a] he's [,] just anoying [n].

Normaly [l], you find him lieing [y] on his bed with a sosage [au] sandwich [x]. televishun [T] [io] and computer [e] games are the most importent [a] things in his life, and the only way to get his attenshun [tion] is to hide the remote.

Now, he has invented this grand sceme [h] to be a sporting supperstar. What an idea [x]! "I'm going to be in the olimpics [Oly]," he says. "I will probabley be a gold medalist [l]." is [I] he sereous [i] [x]?

Much to our surprize [s], he's [,] now taken up exersice [cise] and keeps flexing his mussles [c] at the nieghbors [ei] [u] [x]. if [I] that wasn't bad enugh [o], we now find my brother's [,] horrable [i] sports kit everywhere [x]. its [I] begining [n] to get on my nerves [x]. am [A] I being unreasonable [x]?

Section 1 tasks summary

A Warm-up

Write two sentences and a question using these words only.

ready finally was she

1. She was finally ready.

2. Finally, she was ready.

3. Was she finally ready?

4. Write a question with a different adverb.

   Was she really ready?

Write two words with the ending given.

5. **que**   antique   unique

6. **gue**   tongue   league

7. **cue**   rescue   barbecue

Underline the suffix that you **cannot** add to the word in **bold**.

8. **origin**   al ate <u>able</u> s

9. **act**   ive or <u>ist</u> tion

10. **forgive**   able ness ing <u>tion</u>

> **PART A Focus**
> **1–4:** word order; punctuation
> **5–7:** spelling patterns
> **8–10:** adding suffixes

B Word work

1. The same four-letter string is missing from all these words. Write it in.

   s h **ould** e r s   b **ould** e r   m **ould**   c **ould**

2. The same three-letter string is missing from all these words. Write it in.

   a w k **war** d   r e **war** d   c o **war** d   s **war** m

Add prefixes and suffixes to make a word family.

3. script **ure**   **Clue:** holy writings

4. **pre** script **ion**   **Clue:** for medicine

5. **post** script   **Clue:** PS

6. **in** script **ion**   **Clue:** on a gravestone

7. The root word **script** means   written   .

Write a definition of the word or words in **bold**.

8. **Score** along the dotted lines.

   score: mark with something sharp

9. He listened to **heavy metal**.

   heavy metal: a type of music

10. It changed the **pitch** of the sound.

    pitch: a high or low sound

> **PART B Focus**
> **1–2:** common letter strings
> **3–7:** root words and word families
> **8–10:** inferring meaning from context

C Sentence work

Complete this sentence to make Joe sound

1. **happy**   "Listen to this," chuckled Joe, with a twinkle in his eye.

2. **shocked** "Listen to this," gasped Joe, staring at the letter in amazement.

3. **worried** "Listen to this," muttered Joe, with a furrowed brow.

Cross out the noun phrases and replace them with proper nouns.

4. ~~That player~~ plays for ~~that team~~.   Ben Earl, Woodfield Town

5. I saw ~~a woman~~ going into ~~a shop~~.   Anna, Fay's Deli

6. ~~This man~~ is in charge of ~~this organisation~~.   Mr Jenkins, Sunshine Foods

> **PART C Focus**
> **1–3:** sentences combining direct speech and actions
> **4–6:** proper nouns for precision; capital letters
> **7–10:** use of brackets for a parenthesis

Insert a pair of brackets in the correct place in the sentence. Explain why they are needed.

7. Fold the corners into the centre (see Diagram 2). To separate the note about the diagram.

8. Nelson (1758–1805) was a famous sea admiral. To separate the extra piece of information.

9. Foxes live in many urban (built-up) areas. To separate the definition of 'urban'.

10. Sally (whom I never did trust) went straight to the teacher. To separate the extra comment/ relative clause.

(X) DEFINITIVE ANSWER   (X) SAMPLE ANSWER

A Warm-up

Rewrite the sentence, first as a command (C) and then as a question (Q).

Amy, the pizza is in the oven.

1 C: Put the pizza in the oven, Amy.

2 Q: Amy, is the pizza in the oven?

Make three words by adding prefixes and/or suffixes to the word **skill**.

3 unskilled   5 skilful

4 skillfully

Write three words that end with the suffix.

6 govern ment   docu ment   orna ment

7 hero ic   com ic   poet ic

Put the letters in order to make a word.

8 **l g h a u**   laugh

9 **e g h i w**   weigh

10 **e g h n o u**   enough

B Word work

Add the missing vowels.

1 e x c e l l e n t

2 d e v e l o p

3 p r i v i l e g e

Add one letter to make another word that sounds the same.

4 lightning   lightening

5 bred   bread

Use the words to complete the sentences.

6 The sky seems to be lightening up now.

A fork of lightning cut across the sky.

7 The farmer bred prize-winning cows.

I prefer wholemeal bread.

8 Underline the root word.

perilously triumphantly

Write a definition.

9 **perilously**   dangerously

10 **triumphantly** showing great happiness

C Sentence work

Continue the sentence using one of these relative pronouns.

who that which

1 Once there was a poor farmer who had only one skinny cow.

2 They came to the narrow track that wound its way up to the castle.

3 They huddled round the fire , which was fading fast.

4 George was a stonecutter who lived in a little cottage on the edge of the wood.

Some words have been crossed out. Write new words that sound more positive.

5 a peculiar house with cramped rooms and many old features unique   cosy   original

6 a nosy little girl with a prying mind and sharp eyes   curious   questioning   bright

7 the odd woman with gaudy jewellery and strange hair   quirky   bright   interesting

Add two commas.

8 Once cool, press the beetroot through a sieve, collecting the liquid in a container.

9 Smiling contentedly, Sarah sank into the armchair, glad to be home at last.

10 Before you know it, we will be back to school, James.

A Warm-up

Complete the subordinate clause.

1. Dan did not speak although *everyone was waiting.*

2. Dan did not speak until *the room was silent.*

3. Dan did not speak in case *someone was listening.*

Add one letter to make a homophone.

4. isle *aisle*
5. led *lead*
6. rein *reign*
7. father *farther*

PART A Focus
1–3: subordinate clauses
4–7: homophones
8–9: spelling patterns
10: plural spelling rules

Add the same short word to complete all three longer words.

8. a v e r *age*   s a v *age*   c o u r *age*
9. h a r b *our*   v a p *our*   r u m *our*

10. Change the words into plurals.

factory *factories*   **marsh** *marshes*

industry *industries*   **valley** *valleys*

B Word work

Add a single **t** or double **t**.

1. a *tt* r a c t   a *t* l a s   a *tt* a c h

Add a single **c** or double **c**.

2. a *cc* o u n t   a *cc* u s e   a *c* o r n

Add a single **p** or double **p**.

3. a *p* a r t   a *pp* r o v e   a *p* o l o g y

Add a single **d** or double **d**.

4. a *d* j u s t   a *d* v a n c e   a *dd* r e s s

Complete the phrase with a word formed from the word in **bold**.

5. **sphere**   a *spherical*   shape
6. **resist**   air *resistance*
7. **real**   virtual *reality*

Add the missing noun to the well-known phrase.

8. as fit as *a fiddle*
9. as cool as *a cucumber*
10. as blind as *a bat*

PART B Focus
1–4: double and single consonants
5–7: word structure; related words
8–10: figures of speech

C Sentence work

Nearly every house in the street had a green door. One had a bright red door.

1. What does the pronoun 'one' refer to in the second sentence? *a house*

Complete the sentence that follows on, using the pronoun.

2. Some people agreed with the suggestion. Others *were against the idea.*

3. Ellie made cupcakes to sell on her stall. These *proved to be very popular.*

4. We managed to catch some of the balloons. Many *were blown away by the wind.*

Complete the sentences with a relative clause.

5. They came to a river, which *stretched across the countryside like a ribbon.*

6. His eyes were giant headlights that *shone in the darkness.*

7. They were lost in the fog that *spread over the moorland like a veil.*

PART C Focus
1–4: using pronouns for cohesion
5–7: relative clauses
8–10: commas after fronted adverbials; checking misuse of commas

Cross out any unnecessary commas.

8. One night, as he lay asleep~~,~~ under the stars, Angelo had~~,~~ a dream.

9. For several minutes, the wizard looked~~,~~ at him~~,~~ in silence.

10. Hurriedly, the old woman~~,~~ hid the food~~,~~ in the woodpile, hoping no-one~~,~~ would look there.

Ⓧ DEFINITIVE ANSWER   Ⓧ SAMPLE ANSWER

A Warm-up

Write a sentence using one of these adverbs.

entirely relatively importantly

1. He was entirely wrong.
2. It was a relatively small increase.
3. More importantly, he won the cup.

4. Make six words using these letters only.

   e i g h n r v

   neigh, vein, reign, heir, vine, nigh

Remove one letter to make a new word.

5. brought   bought
6. fought   ought
7. through   though

> **PART A Focus**
> 1–3: adverbs to clarify
> 4: spelling
> 5–7: letter string **ough**
> 8–10: able and ible

Underline the correct spelling.

8. flexable flexeble <u>flexible</u>
9. reversable reverseble <u>reversible</u>
10. <u>forgivable</u> forgiveble forgivible

B Word work

Underline the word that is **not** a real word.

1. autograph automobile <u>autonature</u>
2. microscope <u>microbitus</u> microphone
3. <u>telecut</u> telephone telescope

> **PART B Focus**
> 1–3: word roots
> 4–7: homophones
> 8–10: spelling patterns; words that are often confused

Write the correct homophone.

4. a decorative **freeze**   frieze
5. a **sauce** of information   source
6. pay by **check**   cheque
7. a chest of **draws**   drawers

Add **cy** or **sy** to spell the words correctly.

8. cy l i n d e r   cy m b a l   cy n i c a l
9. sy s t e m   sy m b o l   sy l l a b l e

10. Use two of the words to complete these sentences.

    I can play the ___cymbal___ .

    The dove is a ___symbol___ of peace.

C Sentence work

Continue the sentence with a subordinate clause.

1. He stopped suddenly as if he'd been frozen.
2. Suddenly darkness descended as though a light had been switched off.
3. He would continue his search as long as the rain held off.
4. Amanda escaped as soon as the wizard turned his back.

Sort the adjectives into two groups that could be used to describe a character.

uncaring generous bold snivelling devious feeble dependable cheerful

5. **appealing**   generous, bold, dependable, cheerful
6. **unappealing**   uncaring, snivelling, devious, feeble

Cross out the incorrect words in the sentence.

7. That house on the corner is **theirs** ~~theres their's~~.
8. I believe ~~their there~~ they're on holiday in **their** ~~there they're~~ caravan.
9. These papers are **hers** ~~her's hers'~~.
10. I believe this is **yours** ~~your's~~. I shall put it in **your** ~~you're~~ folder.

> **PART C Focus**
> 1–4: subordinate clauses; using a range of conjunctions
> 5–6: words chosen for effect
> 7–10: possessive pronouns and possessive determiners; correct use of apostrophes

X DEFINITIVE ANSWER   X SAMPLE ANSWER

A Warm-up

Try walking instead of using the car.

Present this idea as a

1. **command**   Don't use the car. Walk instead.

2. **question**   Could you walk instead of using the car?

3. **slogan**   Use your feet, not the car!

Change one letter to make a homophone. Write the new word and its meaning.

4. **peek** (a look)   peak (the top)

5. **steel** (a metal)   steal (take)

6. **sun** (a star)   son (a male child)

PART A Focus
1–3: types of sentence
4–6: homophones
7–10: word structure

Add different endings to complete the three words.

7. pack et   pack age   pack ing

8. press ing   press ure   press ed

9. assist ed   assist ant   assist ing

10. medic al   medic ine   medic ation

B Word work

1. Add **ing** to these verbs.

rebel ling   develop ing   regret ting

2. Add **ed** to the same verbs.

rebel led   develop ed   regret ted

3. Complete these word sums.

rebel + ious = rebellious

regret + able = regrettable

Add the ending **ious** to these words.

4. **malice**   malicious

5. **grace**   gracious

6. **space**   spacious

PART B Focus
1–3: rules for adding suffixes
4–8: words ending cious
9–10: antonyms

7. What do you notice?

The ending makes a 'shus' sound.

8. Write another word that ends with the same spelling.

delicious

Underline the antonym of the word in **bold**.

9. **prosperous**   wealthy <u>poor</u> affluent

10. **trustworthy**   <u>dishonest</u> reliable solid

C Sentence work

Rewrite the sentence, rearranging the adverbials. Use the correct punctuation.

1. Everyone celebrated except Prince James when Princess Agnes was born.

When Princess Agnes was born, everyone except Prince James celebrated.

2. Many years ago there lived a dragon named Jem in a kingdom by the sea.

Many years ago, in a kingdom by the sea, there lived a dragon named Jem.

3. The doors flew open suddenly just as everyone was sitting down to eat.

Just as everyone was sitting down to eat, the doors suddenly flew open.

Cross out the words that are wrong in the sentence. Write the Standard English words.

4. I ~~seen~~ him pick up the book ~~what~~ was lying on the floor.   saw, that

5. I planted ~~them~~ bulbs and ~~done~~ some weeding.   those, did

6. They ~~was~~ not afraid although they did not have ~~no~~ shelter.   were, any

7. The man must ~~of took~~ the money ~~what~~ was on the table.   have taken, that

PART C Focus
1–3: sentence structure; fronting adverbials; commas after fronted adverbials
4–7: Standard English
8–10: expanding nouns

Expand the noun to describe a character that fits the type of story.

8. **legend**   a brave   knight   on a difficult quest

9. **horror**   the gruesome   monster   from the swamp

10. **school story**   the strictest   teacher   at Minford School

   X DEFINITIVE ANSWER   **X** SAMPLE ANSWER

English Skills 4 Answers

A Warm-up

Continue the sentence with a subordinate clause.

1 **She spoke as if** she knew someone was listening.

2 **He crouched down as though he was** trying to hide.

3 **They would remain there as long as** the king allowed.

These words and prefixes are mixed up. Write the words correctly.

megamarket **super**cab **mini**phone

PART A Focus
1–3: using conjunctions
4–7: prefixes
8–10: spelling strategies

4 megaphone

6 supermarket

5 minicab

7 Write three words using the prefix **super**.

supersonic, superstar, superglue

Add the missing letters.

Clue: the name of a different family member completes each word

8 h a u n t e d

10 s m o t h e r

9 s e a s o n a l

B Word work

1 Add the correct ending.

cious tious

deli cious   cau tious   vi cious

Write three onomatopoeic words that might describe the sounds made by

2 **an old car**   rattle, creak, chug

3 **water**   splash, splosh, slosh

4 **animals**   oink, moo, quack

5 Add the correct prefix.

dis mis over re

mis **understand**   over **come**

re **bound**   dis **close**

6 What class do these words belong to? Tick one.

adjectives   nouns   verbs ✓

Write an adjective beginning with the prefix.

7 in visible

8 ir responsible

9 il legal

10 im possible

PART B Focus
1: words ending tious, cious
2–4: onomatopoeia
5–6: prefixes with verbs; word class
7–10: prefixes: in, ir, il, im

C Sentence work

Rewrite the two sentences as one sentence using a subordinate clause.

1 **Joe reached the top. He shouted down.** When Joe reached the top, he shouted down.

2 **He looked in the box. Dad had warned him not to.**
He looked in the box even though Dad had warned him not to.

3 **The little goat trotted down the road. He munched a few leaves.**
As the little goat trotted down the road, he munched a few leaves.

Draw arrows to show where two dashes should go in the sentence.

4 Everything ↑ the walls, the floor and the furniture ↑ was made of glass.

5 Many sports ↑ such as running or swimming ↑ require little equipment.

6 Jess ↑ my little sister ↑ always wants to play pirates.

7 Finally ↑ at the last possible moment ↑ George arrived.

PART C Focus
1–3: combining sentences using subordinate clauses
4–7: dashes to indicate a parenthesis
8–10: Standard English

Cross out the words that are wrong in the sentence. Write the Standard English words.

8 I ~~done~~ the shopping while you ~~was~~ asleep.   did, were

9 If they ~~was~~ hungry they could help ~~theirselves~~ to the sandwiches.   were, themselves

10 I could ~~of~~ give you ~~me~~ spare trainers.   have, given, my

X DEFINITIVE ANSWER   X SAMPLE ANSWER

A Warm-up

Write two adverbs that give different effects.

1. He spoke _nervously_ / _confidently_ .

2. She reacted _calmly_ / _angrily_ .

3. _Hurriedly_ / _Carefully_ , he gathered the papers together.

4. The same five-letter string is missing from all these words. Write it in.

   d _aught_ e r   d r _aught_   c _aught_

Add a three-letter word to complete the longer word.

5. g u a _ran_ t e e

6. o c _cup_ y

7. r e _cog_ n i s e

Add a root word to make a longer word.

8. un _avoid_ able

9. re _place_ ment

10. en _danger_ ed

PART A Focus
1–3: choosing words for effect
4: letter strings
5–7: spelling tricky words
8–10: word structure

B Word work

Add the correct ending.

tial cial

1. par _tial_   offi _cial_

2. spe _cial_   essen _tial_

PART B Focus
1–2: words ending tial, cial
3–4: root words
5–10: meaning of homonyms

Write two nouns that can be formed from the verb.

verb	nouns	
3. **manage**	_manager_	_management_
4. **compete**	_competition_	_competitor_

Write sentences showing the two different meanings of the word.

5. **fan** _He is a Leeds United fan._

6. **fan** _We need a fan to keep cool._

7. **current** _My current score is 10._

8. **current** _The wire carries a current._

9. **overall** _He did well overall._

10. **overall** _He wears an overall at work._

C Sentence work

Expand the notes into a complete sentence.

1. **no Sun = no life on Earth** _Without the Sun, there would be no life on Earth._

2. **hibernate – survive winter** _Some animals hibernate in order to survive winter._

3. **gold metal value** _Gold is a metal that has great value._

Add words that give the two characters opposing characteristics.
Write the type of word you have added.

nouns verbs adjectives adverbs

4. The ladybird _hurried_ and _scurried_ . The grasshopper _dozed_ in the sun. _verbs_

5. Jon was _sociable_ and _cheerful_ . His wife was _selfish_ and _grumpy_ . _adjectives_

6. The Red Knight fought _bravely_ . The Green Knight trembled _fearfully_ . _adverbs_

Underline the information that is **not** essential to the sentence. Add commas to separate it.

7. Neptune, one of the gas giants, is the eighth planet from the Sun.

8. Many stringed instruments, such as the violin, are played with a bow.

9. Hares, like rabbits, have long ears and powerful hind legs.

10. The iguanadon, which is a herbivore, can be 10 metres long.

PART C Focus
1–3: using a variety of sentence structures to explain or define
4–6: choosing words for effect; identifying word classes
7–10: commas to indicate a parenthesis

Ⓧ DEFINITIVE ANSWER   Ⓧ SAMPLE ANSWER

A Warm-up

1. Explain why the headline writer used the word in **bold**.

   "I was **framed**," says art thief.

   Because it has two meanings (framing a picture or making it look like he stole the paintings).

Complete the sentence with a

2. **relative pronoun**

   This is Joe ___who___ lives next door.

3. **possessive pronoun**

   I think this is ___yours___ .

4. **personal pronoun** Did you see ___her___ ?

Add one letter to make the homophone.

5. not ___knot___   6. ring ___wring___

Write a noun related to the adjective.

7. **aggressive**   aggression

8. **determined**   determination

Write the noun as a plural.

9. one **wolf** → two ___wolves___

10. one **goose** → two ___geese___

PART A Focus
1: word meanings
2–4: types of pronoun
5–6: homophones
7–8: related words
9–10: plurals

B Word work

Add the missing letter **s** or **c**.

1. s i n c e r e   i n c i d e n t   i n s t a n t

2. m i s s i l e   c a p a c i t y   m e d i c i n e

3. s u f f i c e   s a c r i f i c e   p r o m i s e

PART B Focus
1–3: spelling patterns; common errors
4–7: verb prefixes
8–10: onomatopoeia

Add the same prefix to all three words to make new verbs.

4. de mist   de compose   de frost

5. dis mount   dis connect   dis mantle

6. mis judge   mis lay   mis behave

7. un block   un wrap   un ravel

Write three onomatopoeic words to suit each setting.

8. **building site**   clatter, thud, crash

9. **deserted house**   creak, squeak, click

10. **riverbank**   gurgle, plop, splash

C Sentence work

Continue the sentence in the style of a traditional story. Add a relative clause.

1. The king was proud of his daughter, whose name was Sophia.

2. They came to a third door, which was even smaller than the other two.

3. There was once a tiger who thought he was the king of the jungle.

Is the question asking for a statement of fact or opinion?

4. When was the king born?   fact

5. Are cars better than bikes?   opinion

6. Are lions bigger than cheetahs?   fact

7. What did you think of the film?   opinion

Cross out the incorrect words in the sentence.

8. Do you know ~~whose~~ who's coming?

9. Do you know whose ~~who's~~ book this is?

10. ~~Whose~~ Who's this? It's the boy whose ~~who's~~ dog we found.

PART C Focus
1–3: narrative style; relative clauses
4–7: fact and opinion
8–10: common confusions using apostrophes

X DEFINITIVE ANSWER   X SAMPLE ANSWER

A Warm-up

Rewrite each sentence using adverbials to say **when**, **where** and **what for**.

1 He begged. *In the morning, he begged for a few crusts at the palace kitchen.*

2 He travelled. *For many years, he travelled the world looking for the lost treasure.*

Join the prefix to its meaning.

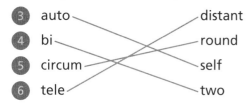

3 auto — two
4 bi — self
5 circum — distant
6 tele — round

PART A Focus
1–2: using adverbials to add detail
3–6: meaning of prefixes
7: related words
8–10: unstressed vowels in words that are often misspelt

7 Write four words related to the root word **create**.
creative, creation, creator, recreate

Add the missing vowels.

8 m i n u t e s   10 i n d i v i d u a l

9 f a m i l i a r

B Word work

1 Add the missing letter **g** or **j**.
s u b j e c t   m a r g i n   f r a g i l e

2 Add the missing letters in these words.
s u g g e s t i o n   g e n u i n e
j u d g e m e n t

3 Add the missing letter **c** or **s**.
o c e a n   a n c i e n t   l e i s u r e

Underline the correct spelling.

4 forsible forcable <u>forcible</u>

5 furyous furrious <u>furious</u>

6 humorus <u>humorous</u> humourous

PART B Focus
1–2: j sound spelt g
3: sh/ch sound spelt c
4–6: spelling rules for adding suffixes and exceptions
7–10: antonyms

Write two antonyms for each word.

7 **love**   *hate, loathe*

8 **good**   *bad, poor*

9 **soft**   *hard, tough*

10 Underline the word that has no opposite.
happy <u>red</u> bright little

C Sentence work

Continue the sentence with a subordinate clause to explain why.

1 Every year thousands of trees are cut down *so that they can be made into paper.*

2 Water is essential to life on Earth *because plants and animals would die without it.*

3 Yeast is often added to bread *in order to make the bread rise.*

4 Myths are called traditional stories *because they are passed from generation to generation.*

Rewrite the sentence, replacing the common noun in **bold** with a longer, more descriptive noun phrase.

5 He saw a **man**.   *He saw a strange little man with red hair.*

6 A **woman** stood nearby.   *An old woman with a woollen shawl stood nearby.*

7 He saw a **man**.   *He saw a police officer with a walkie-talkie.*

8 A **woman** stood nearby.   *A smart young woman in designer clothes stood nearby.*

Add commas, full stops and capital letters so that these sentences make sense.

9 Holding on to the side, he kicked his legs. T the boat moved.

10 Tess smiled. H her mother, whose name was Lucy, laughed out loud.

PART C Focus
1–4: expanding sentences to explain
5–8: expanded noun phrases
9–10: commas, full stops and capital letters

X DEFINITIVE ANSWER   X SAMPLE ANSWER

A Warm-up

Emily admits she was wrong.

Rewrite the sentence using

1 past tense

Emily admitted she was wrong.

2 a perfect verb form

Emily has admitted she was wrong.

3 direct speech

"I was wrong," admitted Emily.

4 an adverb

Finally, Emily admits she is wrong.

5 a different type of sentence

Will Emily admit she was wrong?

6 Make the noun into a verb.

breath *e*   half *ve*

cloth *e*

> **PART A Focus**
> **1–5:** verb tenses; sentence types; punctuation
> **6:** words that are often confused
> **7–10:** spelling strategies

Add the missing syllable or syllables.

7 ske *le* ton   **Clue:** *bones*

8 pe *cu* li *ar*   **Clue:** *strange*

9 a *ston* ish *ment*   **Clue:** *surprise*

10 pre *dic* tion   **Clue:** *forecast*

B Word work

1 Add the missing letters.

s u s p i *c* i o u s   s u p e r s t i *t* i o u s

a n *x* i o u s   f e r o *c* i o u s

c o n s *c* i o u s

2 Add the same ending to all three occupations.

opti *cian*   electri *cian*   mathemati *cian*

Write two more occupations with the same ending.

3 *musician*

4 *magician*

> **PART B Focus**
> **1:** words ending **tious, cious** and exceptions
> **2–4:** words ending **cian**
> **5–8:** common roots; word meanings
> **9–10:** verb prefixes

Write a definition.

5 **transform** *change completely*

6 **translate** *write in a different language*

7 **transport** *move, carry*

8 Write four more words with the root **trans**.

transplant, transfer, transmit, transfix

Add the prefix to complete all three verbs.

9 *inter* **rupt**   *inter* **fere**   *inter* **act**

10 *sub* **merge**   *sub* **scribe**   *sub* **mit**

C Sentence work

Reorder the words in the sentence so that it starts with an adverbial.

1 The duchess looked down sadly on the little town from up in her tower.

From up in her tower, the duchess looked down sadly on the little town.

2 The film star came through the door accompanied by two men.

Through the door, accompanied by two men, came the film star.

3 He ran to the door immediately on hearing the footsteps.

On hearing the footsteps, he immediately ran to the door.

Write a sentence using the three words as pronouns.

4 **he him someone** *As Spencer left the shop, he thought someone was watching him.*

5 **they we ourselves** *We grew the plants ourselves and they all seem to be very healthy.*

6 **she her any** *Mum made the cakes for her but she didn't want any.*

7 **this mine yours** *This is my attempt but yours looks even better than mine.*

Add a parenthesis into the sentence to give extra information.

8 People might laugh at him *– and they did –* but he wasn't worried.

9 Some trees *(called evergreens)* do not lose their leaves in autumn.

10 Everyone *– well, almost everyone –* was delighted with the result.

> **PART C Focus**
> **1–3:** reordering sentences; fronted adverbials
> **4–7:** pronouns
> **8–10:** adding and punctuating a parenthesis

X DEFINITIVE ANSWER   **X** SAMPLE ANSWER

A Warm-up

1 Continue the sentence so that it is at least 20 words long.

Suddenly he stopped *chopping the wood and looked around him, as if waiting for someone or something to appear out of the shadows of the night.*

Write the antonym.

2 **forward** *backward*

3 **increase** *decrease*

4 **fearful** *fearless*

> **PART A Focus**
> **1:** extending sentences
> **2–4:** forming antonyms
> **5–6:** able and ible
> **7–10:** spelling strategies

5 Write four words that end with **able**.

capable, reliable, adorable, probable

6 Write four words that end with **ible**.

visible, terrible, sensible, flexible

Add the missing letters.
Clue: *the name of a different part of the body completes each word*

7 arm o u r

9 s ear c h

8 s u r face

10 p o t a toes

B Word work

Underline the correct spelling.

1 vejetable <u>vegetable</u> vegetible

2 critisise <u>criticise</u> criticice

3 gorjous gorgous <u>gorgeous</u>

> **PART B Focus**
> **1–3:** j sound spelt g; s sound spelt c
> **4–6:** word meanings; context
> **7–10:** figures of speech

Write a definition of the word in **bold**, found on a food safety poster.

4 **hygienic** *clean, free of germs*

5 **disposable** *throwaway*

6 **contaminated** *infected*

In your own words, rewrite the phrase in **bold**.

7 If you **put your foot in it** you *make a blunder.*

8 If you **put your feet up** you *take a rest.*

9 If you **put your foot down** you *go faster/insist/say no.*

10 If you **have your feet on the ground** you *are practical.*

C Sentence work

Combine the three sentences into one. Use a relative clause in each sentence.

1 The man had magic shoes. The man wore the shoes every day. The shoes wore out.

The man had magic shoes, which he wore every day until they wore out.

2 Ursula sold all her hats. She kept one hat. This one hat was Ursula's favourite.

Ursula sold all her hats except one, which was her favourite.

3 Out came an old man. The old man walked down the path. The path led to the village.

Out came an old man who walked down the path that leads to the village.

Add noun phrases to give detailed information.

4 Some jellyfish have *rows of tentacles* that can give a *painful sting.*

5 Crocodiles are *large reptiles* found in *the rivers and swamps in tropical regions.*

6 Mercury is the *smallest planet* in *the solar system.*

7 Liverpool is *a large city* in *the north of England.*

Proofread the sentence. Add the missing punctuation and capital letters.

8 Roald Dahl, the author of the Twits, was born in Wales to norwegian parents.

9 As they waited for the chiefs signal, the clocks hands ticked slowly round.

10 Whales are mammals, not fish, they are covered with skin, not scales.

> **PART C Focus**
> **1–3:** sentence formation; using relative clauses
> **4–7:** noun phrases to expand information
> **8–10:** proofreading

X DEFINITIVE ANSWER   X SAMPLE ANSWER

A Warm-up

Complete the sentence.

1 Only as the clock struck thirteen, did they realise something was wrong.

2 Then, from far and near, people began to arrive in the marketplace.

3 By recycling, we can help to save energy and raw materials.

4 Write the verbs in the past tense.

cancel cancelled **excel** excelled

level levelled **marvel** marvelled

Write three verbs that start with the prefix

5 **over** overflow, overhear, overload

6 **sub** subtract, submerge, subscribe

> **PART A Focus**
> **1–3:** sentence construction
> **4:** past tense; rules for adding **ed**
> **5–6:** verb prefixes
> **7–10:** spelling strategies

Add the missing syllable.
Clue: types of writing

7 ex pla nation

8 per sua sion

9 in struc tions

10 nar ra tive

B Word work

Complete the word.

1 ini tial **Clue: first letter of a name**

2 torr ential **Clue: (of rain) very heavy**

3 arti ficial **Clue: made by people**

4 confi dential **Clue: top secret**

> **PART B Focus**
> **1–4:** words ending tial, cial
> **5–6:** common spelling errors
> **7–10:** subject-specific word meanings

Cross out the words that are wrong. Write the correct spellings.

5 I will ~~acheve~~ if I ~~practice~~ ~~regulary~~.

achieve, practise, regularly

6 It will ~~effect~~ ~~halve~~ the ~~communerty~~.

affect, half, community

Write a definition of the word in **bold**, found in an art gallery.

7 **landscape** a picture of scenery

8 **portrait** a picture of a person

Write a definition of the word in **bold**, found in a word-processing program.

9 **landscape** page set out sideways

10 **portrait** page set out downwards

C Sentence work

Add a parenthesis to give extra information. Punctuate it with commas.

1 The man, who was carrying a heavy sack, climbed out of the window.

2 And so, thanks to Prince Alfonso, the land of Safara was free once more.

3 Vitamin C, which is found in fresh fruit and vegetables, helps to repair wounds.

4 Queen Victoria, who became queen in 1837, reigned for 63 years.

Underline the words that make the sentence into a question.

Complete three questions formed in the same way.

5 You want to look inside, <u>don't you</u>?

6 We can look inside, can't we?

7 You know what's inside, don't you?

8 There's nothing inside, is there?

> **PART C Focus**
> **1–4:** using commas to indicate a parenthesis
> **5–8:** questions using question tags
> **9–10:** direct and reported speech

Reporter: Amy, is it true that you are going to live in America?

Amy Starlet: No comment.

9 Write the complete text as reported speech.

Amy Starlet refused to comment on rumours of a move to America.

10 Write the reporter's question as direct speech in a story.

"Amy, is it true that you're going to live in America?" quizzed a reporter.

Remind the pupil to complete Section 2 of the Progress chart on page 46 of the pupil book.

 DEFINITIVE ANSWER  SAMPLE ANSWER

Writing task assessment sheet: The tortoise and the hare

Name: _____   Class/Set: _____

Teacher's name: _____   Date: _____

Sentence structure and punctuation

	Always/often	Sometimes	Never
Sentences are varied in length			
Sentences with more than one clause are used, including relative clauses and a range of conjunctions			
Adverbials (adverbs, phrases and clauses) are used to add detail			
Sentence construction is varied for effect (e.g. fronted adverbials)			
Appropriate use of tense (including progressive and perfect forms)			
Appropriate use of pronouns to aid cohesion			
Expanded noun phrases are used to describe and add detail			
Sentences are demarcated accurately (no comma splice)			
Direct speech is set out and punctuated correctly			
Commas are used to mark phrases and clauses			
Apostrophes are used for contractions and possession			
Commas, brackets and dashes are used for parenthesis			

Composition and effect

Features of a traditional story are used			
Details are used to appeal to readers (e.g. humour)			
Story is shaped into paragraphs			
Adverbials are used to signal shifts in time, place and focus			
Story has a clear plot, setting and characters			
Language is chosen for effect			

Spelling

Knowledge of spelling patterns is applied correctly			
Longer words are correct, including suffixes and endings (e.g. **cious**, **tious**, **cial**, **tial**)			
Correct spelling of words that are often misspelt (e.g. words with soft **c** or **g**)			
Rules for adding prefixes are applied correctly			
Rules for adding verb endings and suffixes are applied correctly			
Spelling of plurals is correct			
Correct choice of homophones			

Completed proofreading task: Fruity fruit salad

Name: _____ Class/Set: _____

Teacher's name: _____ Date: _____

You could make this colorfull fruit salad for a speshal family ocassion. Use whatever fruits are availible. its simply delishious.

1. Peel, core and chop two avrage-sized apples and immedatly toss them in lemon joose. When using knifes, always ask an adult to help.

2. Desseed the grapes, half the strawberrys and brake sevral satsuma's into segments.

3. Place all the fruit in a large bowl, not forgeting any joose collected during preperation, and stir thoraghly.

4. Carefully, meassure out the orange joose (about 100ml) and pour over the fruit.

5. Slice two kiwi fruit for deceratoin.

6. Leave for about 20 minutes, just long enugh to let the flavors combine. Once ready, serve to you're gests. its a garantteed winner and sure to become your families favorite desert.

Section 2 tasks summary

A Warm-up

Write four sentences using these words only.

into swiftly the rode he night

1. He rode swiftly into the night.
2. Into the night, he rode swiftly.
3. Swiftly, he rode into the night.
4. Into the night, he swiftly rode.

Add the missing letters to spell a word.

5. p h a **ntom**
6. p h o **nics**
7. p h e **asant**

> **PART A Focus**
> **1–4:** reordering sentences
> **5–7:** spelling patterns
> **8–10:** suffixes

Add the same suffix to all three words.

8. poison **ous** prosper **ous** hazard **ous**
9. miser **able** respect **able** suit **able**
10. tropic **al** origin **al** nature **al**

B Word work

Complete the word sum.

1. **shovel** + **ing** = shovelling
2. **excel** + **ent** = excellent
3. **marvel** + **ous** = marvellous
4. What spelling rule did you use?

   Double the final letter 'l' when adding a vowel suffix.

Add the correct prefix.

re dis mis over

> **PART B Focus**
> **1–4:** spelling rules for adding suffixes
> **5–7:** verb prefixes
> **8–10:** using word roots to work out meaning

5. mis **inform**   over **lap**
6. dis **approve**   re **decorate**
7. Which prefix means **do it again**?   re

What does the adjective tell you?

8. an **aquatic** animal

   The animal lives in water.
9. a **futuristic** car

   The car is ahead of its time.
10. stores **nationwide**

    The stores are all over the country.

C Sentence work

Rewrite the three sentences as one. Do this in three different ways.

It was snowing. Mick stayed at home. He kept snug by the fire.

> **PART C Focus**
> **1–3:** varying/selecting sentence structures
> **4–6:** adopting a more formal tone
> **7–10:** punctuating sentences to clarify meaning

1. As it was snowing, Mick stayed at home and kept snug by the fire.
2. It was snowing so Mick stayed at home, keeping snug by the fire.
3. Mick stayed at home and kept snug by the fire, because it was snowing.

Rewrite the sentence so that it sounds more formal, as it would in an informative text.

4. Chimps like leaping around. Chimpanzees are agile, lively animals.
5. Some things stick to the magnet and some jump away.

   Some objects are attracted to the magnet while others are repelled.
6. Too much sugar can give you holes in your teeth.

   Too much sugar can cause cavities to form in your teeth.

Add punctuation to make the meaning clear.

7. Little Jimmy was fed up, too. He sat on the floor, refusing to move.
8. In less than a minute, the entire village vanished. Yes, it vanished into thin air.
9. As the prince rode, he sang to raise his spirits. Of course, he hoped no-one would hear.
10. Amazed at his good fortune, Jas won tickets for the Final. How lucky he was!

X DEFINITIVE ANSWER   X SAMPLE ANSWER

A Warm-up

Complete the sentence to give a different view of the character.

1. "I know," _said_ **Abby,** _comforting_ _him gently._

2. "I know," _screamed_ **Abby,** _banging_ _her fists on the table._

3. "I know," _exclaimed_ **Abby,** _excitedly._

Write a synonymn to use in the story title by replacing the underlined word.

4. The <u>magic</u> piper — _enchanted_

5. The <u>spiteful</u> letters — _malicious_

6. Max the <u>strange</u> — _mysterious_

7. Make three words.

   tele photo ic graph

   telegraph, graphic, photographic

> **PART A Focus**
> **1–3:** constructing sentences; words chosen for effect
> **4–6:** synonyms
> **7–10:** common roots

Draw a line to join the root to its meaning.

8. tele ⟍ to write
9. graph ⟋ light
10. photo ⟋ distant

B Word work

Add the same two letters to complete both words.

1. m e m **o** r y   c a t e g **o** r y

2. i n t e **r** f e r e   l i t e **r** a t u r e

Complete the sentence with an adjective related to the word in **bold**.

3. He has **ambition**. He is _ambitious._

4. He has an **infection**. He is _infectious._

5. I had my **suspicions**. I was _suspicious._

6. **Nutrition** is important. Eat foods that are _nutritious._

> **PART B Focus**
> **1–2:** unstressed vowels in words that are often misspelt
> **3–6:** words ending tious, cious
> **7–10:** formal and informal words

7. Underline the two synonyms that sound most formal.

   lots <u>ample</u> heaps loads <u>sufficient</u> bags

Write two more formal synonyms for

8. **get** _obtain_ _acquire_

9. **give** _provide_ _donate_

10. **tell** _inform_ _notify_

C Sentence work

We can all help to save the planet, starting right now.

Complete the next three sentences by adding relative clauses.

1. Make today the day when _you start to do your bit._

2. After all, Earth is the only planet where _human life can survive._

3. So don't be the person who _helps destroy it._

Write whether you think each statement is **definite** or a **possibility**.

4. I will do that tomorrow.   _definite_

5. I might do that tomorrow.   _possibility_

6. Maybe I'll do that tomorrow. _possibility_

7. I could do that tomorrow.   _possibility_

Add an extra piece of information about the character in a parenthesis. Punctuate it with commas.

8. Simeon _, Sam's evil brother,_ was waiting.

9. Mr Sprott _, the headmaster,_ glared at the young boy.

10. Marianne _, who was sixteen years old,_ liked living in the old house.

> **PART C Focus**
> **1–3:** relative clauses using **where, when, who**
> **4–7:** modal verbs and adverbs to show possibility
> **8–10:** using commas to indicate a parenthesis

A Warm-up

Complete the subordinate clause.

1 He hurried on as if _he were late for an important meeting._

2 He hurried on in case _the robbers caught up with him._

Add the same four-letter word to complete all the longer words.

3 i n t e _rest_ i n g

4 _rest_ a u r a n t

5 a r _rest_ e d

> **PART A Focus**
> **1–2:** using a variety of conjunctions
> **3–5:** spelling
> **6–7:** homophones
> **8–10:** suffixes

Use a pair of homophones to complete the sentence.

6 After a w _eek_ , he was too w _eak_ to move.

7 In the p _ast_ , many laws were p _assed_ .

Add the same suffix to all three words.

8 awe _some_   fear _some_   hand _some_

9 like _wise_   length _wise_   clock _wise_

10 back _ward_   home _ward_   on _ward_

B Word work

Write the word split into syllables. Draw a ring round the vowel that is difficult to hear and makes the word tricky to spell.

1 different   dif / f(e)r / ent

2 preference   pre / f(e)r / ence

3 referee   re / f(e)r / ee

Write the verb that comes from the noun.

4 strength → _strengthen_

5 television → _televise_

6 class → _classify_

7 medicine → _medicate_

8 critic → _criticise_

> **PART B Focus**
> **1–3:** unstressed vowels; spelling strategies
> **4–8:** suffixes to create verbs
> **9–10:** words with more than one meaning

Write a sentence using the word **shed** as a

9 **verb**   _Snakes shed their skin._

10 **noun**   _We keep tools in the shed._

C Sentence work

Add a pair of brackets or dashes in the correct place in the sentence.

1 So Jack swapped Daisy—his mother's favourite cow—for a bag of magic beans.

2 So Jack (the foolish boy) gave away his mother's cow for a pile of magic beans.

Complete these sentences using brackets or dashes in a similar way.

3 So the giant _drank his tea – a whole barrel of it – and then went to sleep._

4 So the giant _(who was really quite rich) started to count his gold coins._

What type of language is used in each sentence? Write **formal** or **informal**.

> **PART C Focus**
> **1–4:** brackets and dashes to indicate a parenthesis
> **5–8:** formal and informal language
> **9–10:** apostrophes for possession

5 I was travelling along Northgate Road when the accident occurred.   _formal_

6 There I was, minding my own business, and guess what happened?   _informal_

Give two reasons for your answers.

7 _5 uses more formal language._

8 _6 sounds more like a conversation._

Add the apostrophes to this magic spell.

9 Mix the spots from four leopards' coats with two wasps' stings and a peacock's feather.

10 Sprinkle with the dust from six butterflies' wings and the shine from a unicorn's horn.

Ⓧ DEFINITIVE ANSWER   Ⓧ SAMPLE ANSWER

A Warm-up

Add an adverbial to the start of the sentence.

1. _Stranded in the desert,_ the men were hungry.

2. _Because there was a famine,_ the men were hungry.

Write four onomatopoeic words.

3. c l ick   c l op   c l atter   c l unk

4. s l am   s l osh   s l urp   s l op

5. c r eak   c r ackle   c r oak   c r unch

Add the ending that sounds like 'shun'. Write the new word.

6. **music** _musician_

7. **corrode** _corrosion_

8. **separate** _separation_

9. **permit** _permission_

10. **circulate** _circulation_

PART A Focus
1–2: fronted adverbials; commas
3–5: onomatopoeia
6–10: words ending cian, sion, ssion, tion

B Word work

1. Underline words with a vowel sound spelt **ei**.

   belief <u>veil</u> achieve shield

   pier <u>rein</u> chief grief

Explain the different spellings.

PART B Focus
1–4: ei and ie spellings
5–7: homophones
8: word structure; prefixes and suffixes
9–10: subject-specific words

2. **ei** is the spelling of a _long 'a' sound_

3. **ie** is the spelling of a _long 'ee' sound_

4. Why is this word different?

   deceive _Because the long 'ee' sound is spelt 'ei' (after 'c')._

Write the word to complete the phrase.

5. a television pro _gramme_

6. a computer pro _gram_

7. a driving lic _ence_

8. Write four words using the root word **act**.

   actor, enact, active, activate

Write a definition of the word **conductor**, as found in

9. **a music book** _leader of an orchestra_

10. **a science book** _a material that conducts heat or electricity_

C Sentence work

Rewrite the sentence so that it gives the same information, but as a **possibility**, not a definite fact.

1. It will be a better day tomorrow. _It could be a better day tomorrow._

2. In the future we will drive electric cars. _In the future we might drive electric cars._

Rewrite the sentence so that it gives the same information, but sounds more **definite**, rather than a possibility.

3. Your money could make a difference. _Your money will make all the difference._

4. Your efforts might help save the planet. _Your efforts will help save the planet._

Complete the sentence using the past perfect form of a suitable verb.

5. The knight _had grabbed_ his sword before he leapt on the white stallion.

6. The beast _had appeared_ from nowhere and was now right in front of them.

7. The fire _had raged_ through the wood, consuming trees as it advanced.

Add the comma needed to make the meaning of the sentence clear.

8. What are you carrying, Ellie?

9. Before leaving, the villagers said their goodbyes.

10. Our team lost, sadly.

PART C Focus
1–4: modal verbs
5–7: use of past perfect verb forms
8–10: commas to avoid ambiguity

X DEFINITIVE ANSWER   X SAMPLE ANSWER

A Warm-up

Write sentences starting with each of these pronouns.

someone something anyone nobody nothing

1. Someone was at the door.
2. Something moved in the shadows.
3. Anyone can join our book club.
4. Nobody dared speak.
5. Nothing could help us now.

Read aloud the list of words. Listen to their sounds.
Underline the odd one out.

6. rough tough <u>plough</u> enough
7. daughter <u>laughter</u> slaughter
8. rein veil <u>either</u> beige

PART A Focus
1–5: pronouns
6–8: letter strings with different sounds
9–10: words with more than one antonym

Underline two antonyms of the word in **bold**.

9. **slow** <u>rapid</u> laze <u>brisk</u> dawdle
10. **light** <u>dim</u> <u>weighty</u> joyful pale

B Word work

1. What punctuation mark is used to join the prefix to the root word?

   non-existent

   colon ___   dash ___   hyphen ✓

2. Write three more words that begin with **non-**.

   non-smoking   non-fiction   non-stop

3. Add a word before **free**.

   fat -free   duty -free   sugar -free

Write the adverb formed from the adjective.

4. **remarkable**   remarkably
5. **impossible**   impossibly
6. **miserable**   miserably
7. **terrible**   terribly

PART B Focus
1–3: use of hyphens
4–7: ably and ibly
8–10: subject-specific words

Give a definition of the word in **bold**, found in notes for a design and technology project.

8. **reinforced** frame   made stronger
9. **mouldable** materials   able to be shaped
10. **compressed** material   squashed down

C Sentence work

Complete the sentence after the adverbial.

1. Along the riverbank, people were waiting for the first boat to appear.
2. Back home, the old lady slept soundly.
3. At the station, Sergeant Green was waiting.

PART C Focus
1–3: adverbials (place)
4–9: identifying grammatical features used in texts
10: commas to avoid ambiguity

Write the text type that each sentence is taken from. Write the grammatical term for the underlined words.

Press the <u>standby button on the remote control</u>.

4. from   an instruction manual
5. It is   a noun phrase.

<u>Clearly</u>, we must stop this from happening!

6. from   persuasive writing
7. It is   an adverb.

Rome, <u>the capital city of Italy</u>, stands on the banks of the River Tiber.

8. from   a report or information text
9. It is   a parenthesis.

10. Explain how the use of a comma changes the meaning in the two sentences.

    No children under ten are allowed.   This means children under ten are not allowed.

    No, children under ten are allowed.   This means children under ten are allowed.

X DEFINITIVE ANSWER   X SAMPLE ANSWER

A Warm-up

Complete the sentence in two ways.

1 In the cold morning air , she shivered and pulled her coat around her.

2 Feeling a little anxious , she shivered despite the sunshine.

PART A Focus
1–2: sentence formation
3–6: spelling strategies
7–10: words from other languages; using a dictionary

Add the missing syllables.

3 di **ges** tion   *Clue: taking in food*

4 **dis** gus **ted**   *Clue: shocked*

5 pre **cau** tion   *Clue: a safety measure*

6 **en** dan **ger**   *Clue: to risk, threaten*

Complete these words from other languages.

7 s p a g **hetti**   *Clue: food (Italian)*

8 k a r **aoke**   *Clue: entertainment (Japanese)*

9 g u i **llotine**   *Clue: a cutting device (French)*

10 d u n **garees**   *Clue: clothing (Hindi)*

B Word work

Add two more words starting with the same letters.

1 Ghana ghastly   ghoulish, ghost

2 rhyme rhino   rhythm, rhombus

3 symbol sycamore   system, sympathy

4 cycle Cyprus   cymbal, cylinder

5 Add **ous**. Check the spelling of the word.

disaster   disastrous

wonder   wondrous

monster   monstrous

6 What do you notice about the spelling?

There is no 'e' in the adjective.

Write the opposite of these maths terms.

7 **ascending**   descending

8 **positive**   negative

9 **probable**   improbable

10 **maximum**   minimum

PART B Focus
1–4: spelling patterns
5–6: exceptions when adding **ous**
7–10: opposites; subject-specific terms

C Sentence work

Use the adverbials to make a coherent case for a Walking Bus scheme.

A Walk to School scheme has many advantages.

1 Firstly, it would help to solve the parking problems outside the school gates.

2 Secondly, it would solve many traffic congestion problems around the school.

3 In addition, it would cut down on harmful pollution.

4 Furthermore, everyone taking part would be much fitter.

Sort these adverbs into those that show certainty and possibility.

clearly definitely maybe obviously perhaps possibly probably surely

5 **certainty**   clearly   definitely   obviously   surely

6 **possibility**   maybe   perhaps   possibly   probably

7 Make this sentence sound more certain.   This is clearly wrong.

Add the punctuation to this dialogue.

8 "I'm 'ungry," moaned the monster, rubbing his stomach.

9 "You've just had breakfast," sighed Jim.

10 "Still 'ungry," moaned the monster. "Very 'ungry."

PART C Focus
1–4: linking adverbials (number, listing)
5–7: adverbs for possibility
8–10: punctuating direct speech; using apostrophes to mark missing letters

X DEFINITIVE ANSWER   X SAMPLE ANSWER

37

A Warm-up

Rewrite the sentence in a more formal way.

1 I ditched the rest.

I disposed of the rest.

2 The film was slated.

The film was not well received.

3 The kids soon perked up.

The children soon cheered up.

Split the word to show the prefix, root and suffix.

4 insincerely   in / sincere / ly

5 unoriginal   un / origin / al

6 especially   e / special / ly

Add a word after the hyphen.

7 hi- tech

8 dog- lover

9 self- service

10 X- ray

PART A Focus
1–3: formal and informal words
4–6: word structure to aid spelling
7–10: use of hyphens

B Word work

Add **ei** or **ie** to make the long **ee** sound.

1 p ie r c e   g r ie f

2 c ei l i n g   c o n c ei t e d

3 What spelling rule did you use?

'i' before 'e' except after 'c'

Add the correct suffix to form nouns. Make sure the noun is spelt correctly.

ism ity

4 hero ism   generous ity

5 sincere ity   critic ism

6 Write the nouns that name special qualities a person might have.

heroism, generosity, sincerity

Write **formal** or **informal** beside each word or phrase.

7 **stuck-up**   informal

8 **arrogant**   formal

9 **understand**   formal

10 **get it**   informal

PART B Focus
1–3: spelling patterns: ei after c
4–6: using further suffixes: ism, ity
7–10: formal and informal synonyms

C Sentence work

Add the word needed to complete the relative clause.

1 This is the place   where   Van Gogh painted his most famous works.

2 That is the girl   whose   painting won the competition.

3 That was the year   when   he was most successful.

Write the sentence with a different modal verb.

4 You will find out a lot about bats.   You should find out a lot about bats.

5 You can help to save the planet.   You might help to save the planet.

6 I must find out more.   I will find out more.

Use two dashes to add a parenthesis into the sentence.

7 Lots of materials   – such as paper –   can be recycled.

8 Everyone   – adults and children –   is welcome to join in the fun.

PART C Focus
1–3: relative clauses beginning with where, when, whose
4–6: modal verbs
7–10: dashes and commas to indicate a parenthesis

Use commas to add a parenthesis into the sentence.

9 William Shakespeare   , the famous playwright,   is well known all over the world.

10 The pyramids   , which are the tombs of the pharoahs,   are amazing buildings.

X DEFINITIVE ANSWER   X SAMPLE ANSWER

A Warm-up

Complete this sentence using different preposition phrases.

1 Oliver waited *by the entrance.*

2 Oliver waited *until midnight.*

3 Oliver waited *with his mother.*

4 Oliver waited *under the clock.*

Add a homophone to complete the joke.

5 **Question:** Which vegetable can sink a boat?

   Clue: it's long, green and white

   Answer: A l e e k !

6 **Waiter:** It's b e a n soup, sir.

   Customer: I don't care what it's b e e n

   before! What is it now?

Add a prefix to make a verb.

7   re ject

8   un earth

9   super vise

10   dis arm

> **PART A Focus**
> **1–4:** preposition phrases
> **5–6:** homophones
> **7–10:** verb prefixes

B Word work

Add the missing vowels. Draw a ring round the vowel sound that is difficult to hear.

1 o f f ⓔ r i n g

2 b u s ⓘ n e s s

3 d e a f ⓔ n i n g

4 w i d ⓔ n i n g

> **PART B Focus**
> **1–4:** spelling strategies; unstressed vowels
> **5–6:** verb suffixes
> **7–8:** word classes
> **9–10:** formal and informal language

Add a suffix and write the new word.

ise ify

5 **magnet**   *magnetise*

6 **sign**   *signify*

7 Underline the word type that describes the root words above.

   <u>nouns</u> adjectives verbs

8 Underline the word type that describes the new words above.

   nouns adjectives <u>verbs</u>

Write a more formal word in place of the word in **bold**.

9 He has **guts**.   *determination*

10 He is **laid back**.   *relaxed*

C Sentence work

Continue the sentence so that it includes a relative clause. Make it sound like a

1 **traditional tale**   She came to *the marble castle where the princess lived.*

2 **fantasy**   She came to *a giant metal cliff, which suddenly opened like a huge sliding door.*

3 **mystery story**   She came to *the end of the corridor, where the secret door was.*

Rewrite the sentence in a more formal way.

4 Loads of people think a new leisure centre would be really cool. *Many local people believe that a new leisure centre would benefit the community.*

5 There's not much else we can do. *There are no real alternatives.*

6 We asked lots of people and nearly everyone said it would be great. *A recent survey shows widespread support for the idea.*

Is the apostrophe used correctly? Put a tick or a cross. Explain your answer.

> **PART C Focus**
> **1–3:** composing sentences with relative clauses
> **4–6:** using formal language
> **7–10:** proofreading: checking use of apostrophes

7 India's monsoon season ✓ *The monsoon season belongs to India.*

8 No-ones' sure. ✗ *It should be 'no-one's', which is the shortened form of 'no-one is'.*

9 "Where are you goin' then, laddy?" he asked. ✓ *'goin'' is a shortened form of 'going'.*

10 Six tree's were chopped down. ✗ *'trees' is a plural, not a possessive noun.*

Ⓧ DEFINITIVE ANSWER   Ⓧ SAMPLE ANSWER

A Warm-up

Write three sentences using the word **flat** as a

① **noun** The parcel was delivered to her flat.

② **adjective** The parcel was flat and square.

③ **adverb** When I walked in, Mark was lying flat on the floor.

Use a different four-letter word to complete each longer word.

***Clue:** each word starts with t*

④ d e term i n e d

⑤ p r o test e d

⑥ a t tent i o n

> **PART A Focus**
> **1–3:** word classes
> **4–6:** spelling strategies
> **7–10:** spelling; using a dictionary

Write a word beginning with these letters.
You can use a dictionary.

⑦ s a b otage   ⑨ s a u sage

⑧ s a c rifice   ⑩ s a p phire

B Word work

Add the suffixes. Write the two new words.

① forgive **en** **able**   forgiven   forgivable

② excuse **ed** **able**   excused   excusable

③ change **ing** **able**   changing   changeable

④ notice **ed** **able**   noticed   noticeable

⑤ What do you notice about adding **able** to the words ending **ge** or **ce**?

They keep the 'e' when adding 'able'.

Cross out the incorrect word in the sentence.

⑥ It was a ten ~~story~~ storey building.

⑦ Blood contains red and white **cells** ~~sells~~.

⑧ A ~~vain~~ vein carries blood to the heart.

⑨ Add the prefix **co** before the hyphen.

co -pilot   co -owner   co -writer

⑩ What does **co** mean?

jointly

> **PART B Focus**
> **1–5:** spelling patterns; adding **able**
> **6–8:** homophones; subject-specific words
> **9–10:** prefixes with hyphens

C Sentence work

Use the dash to add another main clause to the sentence.

① Miss Edgar was very angry – there was steam coming out of her ears!

② Mum took Nikki's side – I knew she would.

③ It rained every day of our holiday – what a surprise!

④ We are going to win the league this year – I hope.

Sort the adverbials into two groups.

on the other hand, certainly, however, clearly, furthermore, in contrast

⑤ **making a case in favour** certainly, clearly, furthermore

⑥ **giving an opposing view** on the other hand, however, in contrast

⑦ Write three more adverbials that you might use to put the case **for** something.

moreover, also, after all

Proofread these sentences. Add punctuation and capital letters.

> **PART C Focus**
> **1–4:** using dashes between independent clauses
> **5–7:** using adverbials to link ideas
> **8–10:** proofreading: adding punctuation

⑧ "Don't!" cried Cyril. "Whatever you do, don't turn round."

⑨ Rajesh, a 26-year-old plumber, told our reporter, "I didn't see the bus until it was too late."

⑩ Jack Spelling's book begins with the line, "Humphrey Norton's life was a mess."

40

Ⓧ DEFINITIVE ANSWER   Ⓧ SAMPLE ANSWER

A Warm-up

1 Write a series of linked sentences.

It began to rain.

Earlier, it had been sunny and warm.

Now, the sky was dark.

Soon, the gutters were filled with

running water.

Complete the word sum.

2 **differ** + ence = difference

3 **refer** + ence = reference

4 **confer** + ence = conference

Complete these compound words.

Clue: all computer terms

5 net work

6 up date

7 down load

8 on line

9 tool bar

10 short cut

> **PART A Focus**
> **1:** cohesion; time adverbials
> **2–4:** adding vowel suffixes
> to words ending **fer**
> **5–10:** subject-specific
> compound words

B Word work

1 Underline the odd one out.

yield brief <u>weird</u> thief piece

2 Why is the odd one out unusual?

Because it contains an 'ei' spelling and

'ie' is more common (except after 'c').

Add the same prefix to both words.

3 pro ject   pro duce   **5** ex ceed   ex cept

4 sus pect   sus pense   **6** en close   en joy

Write a definition of the word in **bold**.

7 Select the **channel** you want to view.

channel: station

8 He was the first to swim the **Channel**.

Channel: the water between England

and France

9 It was a **joint** attempt.

joint: combined

> **PART B Focus**
> **1–2:** spelling patterns **ei** and **ie**
> **3–6:** less common prefixes
> **7–10:** everyday subject-specific words

10 Your wrist **joint** allows you to move
your hand.

joint: where two bones fit together

C Sentence work

These lovely creatures have lived here for centuries but sadly they are now endangered.

1 Which verb is in the present perfect form?   have lived

2 Which phrase shows the writer's view of the creatures?   these lovely creatures

3 Which word shows the writer's opinion of events?   sadly

Continue the sentence above with another sentence showing

4 **certainty**   We must do something to save them.

5 **possibility**   This could be the end for these beautiful creatures.

> **PART C Focus**
> **1–3:** identifying grammatical
> features in texts
> **4–5:** showing possibility/
> certainty
> **6–7:** relative clauses and
> omitted pronouns
> **8–10:** commas

Rewrite the sentence without the relative pronoun.

6 Joe, who is aged ten, won the race.   Joe, aged ten, won the race.

7 This is the book that Dad gave me.   This is the book Dad gave me.

Add two commas.

8 They plunged onwards, pushing deeper into the tunnel, losing all sense of direction.

9 As Sophie sat on the hillside, the wind in her hair, she felt the land tremble beneath her.

10 Apes, unlike monkeys, have no tails.

X DEFINITIVE ANSWER   X SAMPLE ANSWER

A Warm-up

Write two sentences using these words.

doorway darkness

PART A Focus
1–2: conjunctions
3–6: homophones
7–10: more prefixes

Use a different conjunction in each.

1   Azara peeped through the doorway,
    but all she could see was darkness.

2   As she peeped through the doorway,
    Azara waited for her eyes to adjust
    to the darkness.

Write the homophone.

3 **key**   quay   5 **him**   hymn

4 **waist** waste   6 **serial** cereal

Write two words starting with the prefix.

7   **hyper**   hyperlink, hypermarket

8   **inter**   internet, interact

9   **mega**   megalith, megastar

10 **eco**   ecosystem, ecology

B Word work

Complete the word sum.

1   **rely**   + able + ly = reliably

    response + ible + ly = responsibly

Add a prefix before the hyphen.

PART B Focus
1: ably and ibly
2–3: prefixes with hyphens
4–8: suffixes to create verbs
9–10: root words

2   co -operate   non -stick

3   ex -president   semi -final

4   Add a suffix to make a verb.

    active activate   **mobile** mobilise

    simple simplify   **dark**   darken

Use one of the verbs in each sentence.

5   The sky began to   darken   .

6   " Activate   the machine!" said Dr Brains.

7   We need to   simplify   the wording.

8   The king began to   mobilise   his forces.

Write three words from the same word family as the word in **bold**.

9   **horror**   horrify, horrible, horrific

10 **human**   inhuman, humanly, humane

C Sentence work

Look at how the writer has changed this sentence. Explain two changes.

We know this is wrong.   Every right-thinking person knows this is utterly wrong.

1   'Every right-thinking person' makes it sound like everyone thinks this way.

2   The adverb 'utterly' makes it sound more certain.

Rewrite this sentence so that it sounds more definite.

3   **Every child should have a place to live.**   Surely every child must have a safe home.

Complete the simile with a noun phrase.

4 **He moved like** a panther after its prey.   6 **She clucked like** a fussy hen.

5 **Kapil followed like** a lost puppy.   7 **Megan behaves like** a petulant child.

Write this text as direct speech, using a new line each time the speaker changes.

The man wanted to speak to the chief. I asked him to leave, but the man said it was urgent.

PART C Focus
1–2: identifying grammatical features used in texts
3: using adverbs and modal verbs to show possibility
4–7: similes; noun phrases
8–10: punctuating direct speech

8   "I want to speak to the chief," said the man.

9   "I'm sorry, that's not possible. You must leave," I replied.

10 "But I MUST speak to the chief," insisted the man. "It's urgent."

X DEFINITIVE ANSWER   X SAMPLE ANSWER

A Warm-up

Fruit is good for you.

Extend this sentence by adding

1. **a parenthesis** Fruit , such as an apple, is good for you.

2. **another clause** Fruit is good for you so try to eat your five a day.

3. **a dash** Fruit is good for you — it is the perfect snack!

Add a three-letter word to complete the longer word.

4. v o l can o
5. c o m put e r
6. c o m pet i t i o n
7. i n g red i e n t s

PART A Focus
1–3: extending sentences
4–7: spelling strategies
8–10: noun and verb suffixes

Write a noun and a verb related to the adjective.

	adjective	noun	verb
8	**moist**	moisture	moisten
9	**terrible**	terror	terrify
10	**dramatic**	drama	dramatise

B Word work

Add the missing letters.

1. v ei n — *Clue: carries blood*
2. r e c ei v e — *Clue: to be given something*
3. a n c ie n t — *Clue: very old*
4. f ie r c e l y — *Clue: viciously*

Add the suffix **ity** and write the new word.

5. **secure** security
6. **popular** popularity
7. **human** humanity

PART B Focus
1–4: spelling patterns ei and ie
5–8: suffixes: ity
9–10: subject-specific word meanings

8. What type of words have you made? nouns

Write two definitions of the word in **bold**.

9. **table**
   in maths: list of facts and numbers
   another meaning: item of furniture

10. **fast**
    in religious education (RE): a special time when you do not eat
    another meaning: quick

C Sentence work

1. Underline the past perfect verb form. **Oliver sat up suddenly. Something <u>had woken</u> him.**

2. Explain why it is used To refer back to something that happened before.

Complete the sentence using the past perfect form of a verb.

3. The clock had stopped ticking.

4. All the lights had gone out.

Rewrite the sentence, reorganising the clauses.

PART C Focus
1–4: using past perfect verbs
5–7: reordering clauses; commas after fronted adverbials
8–10: punctuation to clarify meaning

5. We need to raise more money to continue our valuable work.
   To continue our valuable work, we need to raise more money.

6. There will be no open spaces left if we continue to build more houses.
   If we continue to build more houses, there will be no open spaces left.

7. They waited for his return while the sun began to sink behind the rooftops.
   While the sun began to sink behind the rooftops, they waited for his return.

Add commas, full stops and capital letters to make the meaning clear.

8. Overall, the film is stunning. From opening scene to thrilling ending, you will be gripped.

9. He looked everywhere. He searched every box, every drawer, every hiding place.

10. We need to raise money. We need your help. Without it, more birds will die.

Remind the pupil to complete Section 3 of the Progress chart on page 46 of the pupil book.

Writing task assessment sheet: Outraged

Name: _____ Class/Set: _____

Teacher's name: _____ Date: _____

Sentence structure and punctuation

	Always/often	Sometimes	Never
Sentences are varied (e.g. varying sentence length and using a range of sentence types)			•
Subordinate clauses are used, including relative clauses, to develop ideas			
Sentence construction is varied for effect (e.g. fronted adverbials)			
Appropriate use of tense, including perfect forms			
Appropriate use of pronouns to aid cohesion			
Modal verbs or adverbs are used to modify opinions or suggest possibilities (e.g. **might**, **possibly**)			
Standard English is maintained			
Sentences are demarcated accurately (no comma splice)			
Commas are used to mark phrases and avoid ambiguity			
Apostrophes are used for contractions and possession			
Commas, brackets and dashes are used for parenthesis			
A single dash is used correctly for effect			

Composition and effect

Clear sense of purpose is shown with features appropriate to persuasive text			
Ideas are organised in separate paragraphs			
Adverbials are used to link sentences and paragraphs			
Language is chosen to enhance persuasion			
Appropriate formal style is used			

Spelling

Knowledge of spelling patterns is applied correctly			
Longer words are correct, using knowledge of syllables and word structure			
Correct spelling of words that are often misspelt			
Correct spelling of a range of prefixes and suffixes			
Rules for adding verb endings and suffixes are applied correctly			
Spelling of plurals is correct			
Correct choice of homophones			

Completed proofreading task: The genie of the bedside lamp

Name: _____ Class/Set: _____

Teacher's name: _____ Date: _____

~~Seen~~ Scene 2: In the living room, ~~what~~ which is a real mess.

Emily: (*in disbeleif* [ie]) What a mess! ~~whats~~ [W] happen[e]d to Dad[']s preshous [ci] CD colection[l]? ~~heel~~ He'll be furious[.]. ~~what~~ [W] will he say?

Ben: (*snappily*) He[']s not going to say ~~nothing~~ anything because it'll be reorgernised [a] when he gets back.

Emily: Are you insane? This is disasterous[.]. ~~your~~ You're definetly [ie] in truble[o]. I sugest [g] you find a good explaination.

Ben: (*sighing*) I shall probebly [a] regret this, but watch…

Ben picks up a table lamp. As he rubs it, there is a deafning [e] roar.
Emily lets out a shreik [ie] as a genie appears, floating by the cieling [ei].

Emily: What is that?

Ben: (*impashently* [ti]) Isn[']t it obveous[i]? It[']s a genie, of coarse [u].

Emily: But that[']s impossable [i], isn[']t it[.]?

Section 3 tasks summary

Full list of Schofield & Sims English Skills books

Pupil books

English Skills Introductory Book	ISBN 978 07217 1402 8
English Skills 1	ISBN 978 07217 1404 2
English Skills 2	ISBN 978 07217 1406 6
English Skills 3	ISBN 978 07217 1408 0
English Skills 4	ISBN 978 07217 1410 3
English Skills 5	ISBN 978 07217 1412 7
English Skills 6	ISBN 978 07217 1414 1

Answer books

English Skills Introductory Book Answers	ISBN 978 07217 1403 5
English Skills 1 Answers	ISBN 978 07217 1405 9
English Skills 2 Answers	ISBN 978 07217 1407 3
English Skills 3 Answers	ISBN 978 07217 1409 7
English Skills 4 Answers	ISBN 978 07217 1411 0
English Skills 5 Answers	ISBN 978 07217 1413 4
English Skills 6 Answers	ISBN 978 07217 1415 8

Teacher's Guide

The teacher's guide contains the **Entry tests**, **Diagnostic checks** and many other useful items suitable for use with the **English Skills** pupil books:

English Skills Teacher's Guide	ISBN 978 07217 1416 5

Also available

Mental Arithmetic is similar in format to **English Skills**, providing intensive maths practice.

For further information about both series, visit the Schofield & Sims website (www.schofieldandsims.co.uk).

Free downloads

A range of free downloads is available on the Schofield & Sims website, including:

- **National Curriculum chart**
- **Entry tests**
- **Entry test group record sheet**
- **Entry test marking keys**
- **Selecting the appropriate pupil book**
- **Achievement award certificates.**